BELIEVER ON SUNDAY, ATHEIST BY THURSDAY

BELIEVER ON SUNDAY, ATHEIST BY THURSDAY

Is Faith Still Possible?

Ronald P. Byars

FOREWORD BY *Jessica Tate*

CASCADE *Books* • Eugene, Oregon

BELIEVER ON SUNDAY, ATHEIST BY THURSDAY
Is Faith Still Possible?

Cascade Books
An Imprint of Wipf and Stock Publishers
199 W. 8th Ave., Suite 3
Eugene, OR 97401

www.wipfandstock.com

PAPERBACK ISBN: 978-1-5326-6745-9
HARDCOVER ISBN: 978-1-5326-6746-6
EBOOK ISBN: 978-1-5326-6747-3

Cataloguing-in-Publication data:

Names: Byars, Ronald P., author. | Tate, Jessica, foreword.
Title: Believer on Sunday, atheist by Thursday : is faith still possible? / Ronald P. Byars; foreword by Jessica Tate.
Description: Eugene, OR: Cascade Books, 2019. | Includes bibliographical references.
Identifiers: ISBN: 978-1-5326-6745-9 (paperback). | ISBN: 978-1-5326-6746-6 (hardcover). | ISBN: 978-1-5326-6747-3 (ebook).
Subjects: LCSH: Spiritual life—Christianity. | Christianity—21st Century. | Discipling (Christianity). | Spirituality.
Classification: BL2525 B93 2019 (print). | BL2525 (epub).

JULY 9, 2019

In appreciation of Pastor Ron Luckey,
friend and colleague in faith,
community organizer, student of Scripture,
servant and preacher of the gospel.

Previous books by Ronald P. Byars

Christian Worship: Glorifying and Enjoying God

The Future of Protestant Worship: Beyond the Worship Wars

The Bread of Life: A Guide to the Lord's Supper for Presbyterians

Lift Your Hearts on High: Eucharistic Prayer in the Reformed Tradition

What Language Shall I Borrow? The Bible and Christian Worship

The Sacraments in Biblical Perspective

Come and See: Presbyterian Congregations Celebrating Weekly Communion

Finding Our Balance: Repositioning Mainstream Protestantism

Contents

Foreword

THERE ARE DAYS WHEN it feels like the world is burning. The community I love grieves another victim of gun violence. The image on the front page of the paper of a malnourished child makes me weep. A friend carries deep pain of abuse in her marriage. These are on the forefront of my mind today.

In the depths of these times, the promises of my faith—that good news comes to the oppressed, that the brokenhearted are bound up, that prisoners find release, that comfort finds those who mourn—are hard to hold onto. I actively remind myself that I have believed these things so fully that I devoted my life to sharing them with others, to serving the church, to nurturing faith, and proclaiming good news.

But the doubt and despair do not relinquish their claim on my gut so easily. And I'm not alone in that. The atheists will point out the foolishness of faith, the ridiculous nature of these claims, the naivety of the religious. The "spiritual but not religious" types are more comfortable with claims like peace and joy than the specific promises of God found in Scripture. Ordinary mainline church members—well educated, successful, literary, scientifically-minded, *New York Times*-reading folks—find ourselves a little embarrassed by these faith claims.

I admit to wondering if these claims can really be trusted—when push comes to shove, when life is on the line, can we really relinquish our own abilities and trust God to make good on these promises? And are we really willing to tell those who face immeasurable suffering that these promises of God can be relied upon? That they can trust these salvation promises scripture so confidently announces?

It seems foolish for the educated to say. Embarrassing for the clear-eyed to believe. Can we really truly trust these promises of comfort and joy in a broken and fearful world? Can we really stake our lives on them?

Ron Byars takes up the question in these pages: is faith possible for a thoughtful person who is paying attention in today's world? And not just any faith, but the classical faith of the ecumenical church: catholic, evangelical, reforming—is it possible today?

Not surprisingly, the answer, Byars concludes, is yes, but it is a well-earned yes as he takes us through the particular challenges confronting a classical faith today.

Byars writes to the faithful of the mainline church who are "between a rock and a hard place" in twenty-first century North America. We are the faithful in the midst of cultural transition. We are a church caught between "an aggressive and reactionary evangelicalism" and religious skepticism. Byars observes that those of us in the mainline "stalk off and leave [faith] to the extremists who seem to have kidnapped the God we thought we knew." Rather than be lumped in with those who push a "cranky Jesus who is big on disapproval," we too often retreat to uncomfortable company with religious skeptics and the quiet, tepid faith that does not offend.

This retreat, while understandable, deadens faith. It forces faith out of the communal and into the individual realm, where it becomes fragile. But more significantly, this retreat places faith into categories of knowledge and understanding that are inappropriate and insufficient to bear the weight of human experience.

Byars brings this to light, outlining constraints that Enlightenment thinking places on our engagement with the world. These constraints, he argues, have flattened our faith from a rich, poetic, precognitive trust to a textbook, literalist explanation of the impossible. While never discounting the benefits of reason and provable data, he reminds us that knowing something to be true occurs not only through detached, reasoned observation, but often more deeply in close proximity, where one has developed a relationship. Likewise, there are aspects of life that are invisible, but perhaps even more important than that which is visible. Byars challenges our conscious understanding of the material world, reminding us that the world around us is not only matter, but is shot through with the glory of God—if we have eyes to see. And most importantly, he calls the faithful back to ourselves, to the imagination and intuitive knowing that give rise to a reality larger (and more grace-filled) than the one that preoccupies us most of the time.

Shifting focus to the church's practice of faith, Byars pushes against a common and palatable reduction of faith to "just love everyone." Such a belief is insufficient in relation to the complexity of particular settings and the selectiveness of human love. He calls the church to task for colonialism in mission, pushing us to embrace a posture of vulnerability, reciprocity, and listening. He asks whether the ecumenically inclined church has been too theologically timid to meet the reasonable expectations of theological substance and serious engagement with core confessional affirmations without embarrassment or apology.

So when Byars asks if faith is possible in today's world, I find he is writing to me.

Unresolved scenes from my own life drift back into focus as I read these pages.

I remember the Saturday evening that our young adult neighbors join us for dinner. Over the course of the meal, one of them asks what I am preaching about the next day. The sincerity surprises me, and my obtuse and churchy answer brushes the question aside. Was the moment of openness missed?

I reflect on navigating conversation with family members—some of whom are of the more literal Christian persuasion and some religious skeptics—about the work that I do, what I believe, and how I choose to live. Do I spend more energy trying not to offend than to tell the stories that ground me and make my faith alive?

I can hear the voice of a colleague saying that he is glad he is close to retiring. "The church as we know it is broken," he said. "Good luck." Is this the best the gospel can offer to those charged with sharing it? Is this the best we can offer the world?

I recall countless church meetings where someone worries over the lack of young families in the church or sheepishly admits that his own adult children do not attend church anymore. Is what the church is offering so banal that it is irrelevant to those around us?

I am reminded of a yoga teacher sharing her experiences with the church community that surrounded her family during a death. She explores the contours of yogic philosophy and Christian practice and invites me to help make sense of her experiences and observations. Am I prepared to have gracious and fitting conversation about Christian doctrine and practice outside the walls of the church?

Byars' work unsettles me as it accurately names those places in which I find myself regularly. At the same time it encourages me that the faith I have been taught and the faith I claim is a viable option in 2019. And it inspires me that the church at her best has the depth of story, theology, and practice to help us live toward wholeness, and righteousness, and peace as individuals and as communities.

As I write, we have just celebrated Christmas and the wild claim that God becomes flesh and the promise that God will come again to make all things new. We turn our attention now to the rhythms of ordinary time and the holy glinting through the mundane of our daily routines. In a few short months, we will again recall the stories of Easter and proclaim—of all foolish things—Christ raised from the dead, despair giving way to hope, death giving way to life. There is no rational sense in these claims and likely never will be.

While I type, my infant son sleeps in the next room. My family is reeling from an unexpected and dire cancer diagnosis. These are particular to me and familiar to many. In the face of new life, in the shadow of looming death, there is an intuition. A fading away of the trite and the vapid. There is the need of Something More. There is need of the stories of God acting in the world to bring good news to the poor and release to the captives. There is need of the promise to make all things new. There is need of faith. There is need of the church to hold, teach, and spread that faith.

In the moments when it seems the world is burning, when doubt creeps into the gut, when the miracle and fragility of life are felt in full, when there are a thousand reasons it may be foolish to set one's faith in God-made-flesh, Byars reminds us that the God proclaimed by the ecumenical church is one who has shown up time and again and made good on promises. Not always in big, dramatic ways, but in the small, day-to-day showing up, in ways we find hard to explain or to prove, but know in our being to be true. That knowing gives us confidence to imagine that in all the places of our lives—in our churches, in our families, in our cities, in our communities, in the quiet doubts that creep into our guts, in all of those places where brokenness, grief, pain, and dead-ends try to force hope into hiding—we may know and trust that the kingdom of God is at hand. God does indeed show up and make good on promises.

Even in our day. Even in our time.

Is faith possible today? I pray to God the answer is yes.

Jessica Tate
Director, NEXT Church
Christmastide 2018

Introduction

For the times they are a-changin'

— BOB DYLAN

How Did It Happen?

Is FAITH STILL POSSIBLE in North America in the twenty-first century? Particularly, Christian faith of the classical, ecumenical sort? What seemed not so very many years ago to be the "normal" state of being in American society is no longer. It was once presumed that it was normal to profess some kind of faith—at least to have enough of a preference that your relatives knew which pastor to call to preside at your funeral. The pastor to be summoned would be likely, statistically speaking, to have been ordained by a Protestant denomination that had been around more or less since colonial times—in today's language, "mainline." Faith in God and in Jesus Christ, at least in moderation, was taken to be not only normal, but admirable. One might feel pride in being a member of a respectable congregation, and run little risk of being embarrassed by the views or behavior of your pastor, church officers, or other members of your preferred church. Certainly there were atheists, but they were usually quiet about it, or covered it up by appearing in church with some regularity, as though, were their skepticism to be known, it would be cause for social ostracism. Parents raised their children to go to church, and they did; and then they raised their own in the church, generation after generation. At least, that is how we have been led to remember it.

Now, not so much. Memories are sweet, for some at least, but of course they leave out some realities with which we are less likely to have been acquainted. They leave out minorities, particularly members of religious minorities such as Muslims, Hindus, Buddhists, Sikhs, and others who lived among us, usually in small numbers, but were simply not visible to the general culture. And, they leave out a large number of people who professed no particular faith and/or did not go to church, and others who did not conform to social norms and quietly went their own way. And, of course, the presence of Jewish people was recognized, but they had good reasons to avoid drawing too much attention to their religious identity.

After the trauma of World War II, returning service people and their families were eager to return to normal. The shock of the conflict contributed to a generally felt need to search for some sense of meaning, and in that era, the most likely place to search for it would be in a church. The new suburbs drew constituencies for new churches, and long established churches grew, too. The numbers were up and kept rising, and society as a whole took on the appearance of piety as Americans identified themselves as the "godly" people threatened by "ungodly" Communists. While it had always seemed that Americans had had a hard time distinguishing between their piety and their patriotism, the two seemed particularly joined at the hip in the 1950s.

However, as early as the 1960s, the steady increases in church membership had already begun to slow, and there even began to be small but noticeable declines in total membership of the older, so-called "mainline" denominations. The sixties were stormy times, in which many of those churches were drawn into the civil rights movement whether by active participation or quiet consent. Their more conservative members, however, were uneasy with what seemed to be politically activist Christianity, and it was not unusual for dissenters to accuse their own denominations of something like betrayal of the gospel (not to mention betrayal of reluctant constituents). In the meantime, so-called "evangelical" churches, which had been marginalized after the Scopes trial and the fundamentalist controversies of the early twentieth-century, emerged from relative silence to draw new attention. For another two or three decades, the evangelical churches continued the growth that had been characteristic of all churches in the 1950s, while mainline Protestants were more clearly than ever in a state of steady numerical decline and a parallel loss of public influence.

Pushing Back and Pushing Back Again

The social movements of the 1960s tended to be anti-institutional, a disposition not unfamiliar to the American psyche, having left its mark on the national character from at least as early as the Revolutionary war. Mainline churches found themselves on the defensive as they became receptive to new perspectives on race, gender equality, and issues related to human reproduction and sexuality. By the late 1970s and early 80s, Jerry Falwell, Ralph Reed, and other evangelical spokespersons were leading powerful movements to defend American society from changes that seemed to threaten traditional values perceived to be under attack. These values, asserted to be biblical, were thus defended as non-negotiable.

With the motivating energy of people who perceived themselves under siege, evangelical leaders began to push back against change. Insisting that the U. S. was and had always been a Christian nation, they struggled to hold the line and, in fact, to return social norms to the conventional views and mores that had preceded the changing perspectives that began to emerge in the upheavals of the sixties. Becoming politically organized, these evangelicals attempted to gain power, for example, on school boards and state school curriculum committees. When successful, they pressed for teaching something called "creation science" alongside the theory of evolution in public schools. They were working from the presumption that the doctrine of creation and the science of evolution were necessarily in conflict, the result of their reading biblical language as though it should be understood the same way as language in a science textbook. When possible, they used the power of curriculum committees to try to direct how U. S. history textbooks should be written, specifically by following traditional and usually uncritical views. Viewpoints shaped by the interests and experiences of various minorities were not much welcomed. They argued before the courts in favor of posting the biblical Ten Commandments in courthouses or parks, presuming that governments should offer support in public spaces to the sacred symbols of religious majorities. They lobbied in favor of organized prayer in public schools for similar reasons, and charged that the absence of Bible reading and prayer in schools was a major cause of crime and social unrest. They supported movements to repeal or undermine Roe v. Wade and judicial findings favoring the rights of homosexual persons, and resisted movements for gender equality.

At first, as the interests of an aroused evangelical movement merged with or served the purposes of politicians, evangelical churches grew larger and stronger. By the early twenty-first century, however, there began to be signs that the fortunes of these churches had peaked. Nearly two decades on, it has become clear that they, too, like the mainline, have begun to show numerical decline. However, they have long since succeeded in displacing the mainline churches in the public eye, including even to redefining how the general public perceives the Christian faith.

Merging Gospel and Flag

Nevertheless, as they began to join the mainline in the relentless trend of falling numbers, they lost none of their determination. Evangelicals are not, of course, all to be described in the same way. For one thing, the evangelicals being described here are mostly white evangelicals rather than black or brown. And, they are those determined to hold on to an image of America as predominantly European, white, and Christian. However, evangelicals exist who do not fit this pattern and whose social views are more likely to resemble those of ecumenical Christians. Nevertheless, the larger group identified by the evangelical label tend to make little distinction between piety and American nationalism. While these evangelicals may very well be highly suspicious and critical of government, they have a sense of tribal identity that is a blend of old-school patriotism and ideological Christianity. The flag and the cross are, in their eyes, not likely to be in tension. Rather, it is presumed that both stand for the same things, i.e., as the identifying emblems of an "exceptional" people, presumed to enjoy God's special favor.

It is possible to be sympathetic with those who feel they have suffered a loss, because large-scale social change tends to be hard. One is tempted to measure social changes in terms of gains and losses, winners and losers, and no one wants to feel themselves on the losing side. But, while social change may develop more rapidly today than it generally has historically, such change has nevertheless always occurred, however gradually. As our horizons expand, we leave behind some social patterns that once served well enough, perhaps even for a very long time. However, the pain of leaving behind can be balanced by the real value of what we are likely to have gained. So, one may feel sympathy, and even share the strain of having to alter comfortable ways of thinking and organizing our lives and relationships. But surely, desperately struggling to return to an earlier time is not the way to go.

We left behind monarchy, slavery, and child labor. We can also leave behind various traditional forms of domination, whether race- or gender-based. We have begun to discover that people who don't fit traditional patterns of sexual identity can only be successfully dehumanized or demonized when we don't know them personally. Once we recognize them among our family and friends and in our congregations, they help us to recognize the variations possible in our complex and shared humanity. The desire to exclude or vilify fades. What seems to have been a loss becomes revealed to be, for most, a gain. Certainly, some old and venerable values have not only been conserved, but also made their own contribution to the formation of newer perspectives, replacing familiar and dearly held prejudices. For example, to conserve biblical faith is to be deeply interested in the protection of the stranger and the vulnerable. The ministry of Jesus is a study in the crossing of otherwise forbidding boundaries based on dividing an "us" from a "them." It might well be argued that the true conservative is the one tuned in to the basic boundary-breaking values embodied in Jesus himself. Still, our age is a time of transition, and transitions involve a certain amount of instability and resulting anxiety.

One of the side effects of the mainline/old-line churches having been rendered nearly invisible by the rise of militant evangelicalism is polarization. In this case, the two most conspicuous extremes of polarization are either aggressive and reactionary forms of evangelicalism, on the one hand, or a bold religious skepticism on the other. Aggressive evangelicalism, attempting to reclaim the nation and culture in order to restore the privileged position of certain kinds of Protestant Christianity, has espoused a stance that tends to be both anti-science and anti-intellectual. It makes no room for adherents of other faiths, people of no faith, or even mainline Protestants. It has been on a quest to reclaim all the public space for itself. The not unexpected effect has been resistance, as measured both by the growing number of people (particularly young people) claiming no religious affiliation, and the normalization of public expressions of religious skepticism. Ecumenical churches ("mainline") that once enjoyed general approval and public respect are puzzled and dismayed to find that they have virtually lost their identity in the confusing collisions of fundamentalisms and hostile skepticism.

Looking for Allies

Mainline Protestants have been part of the resistance to aggressive evangelicalism, of course, but religious skeptics have hit back harder and benefit from a higher profile. Mainline Protestants can mount all sorts of arguments to counter the evangelical right, and sometimes they do, but not so publicly as to be much noticed. Even to follow their arguments requires paying attention to detail as well as a certain degree of sophistication. Not surprisingly, the general public has already lumped all Christians together, considering all of us to be immodest, judgmental, hypocritical, anti-science, and eager to exert power to elbow our way back into dominance of the public space. In short, the mainliners are also neither much understood or much trusted, and their reasoned critiques of the evangelical party capture little attention. The skeptics, however, are less burdened. It is easy enough for them simply to fight back with the weapons at hand, no holds barred. Those weapons include, they imagine, both science and history, while they are spared the need to form nuanced critiques of the way their evangelical opponents read and understand Scripture and Christian doctrine.

Ecumenical Protestants are further handicapped by the fact that they share many things of value with the aggressive evangelicals: faith in God, Christ's incarnation and resurrection, affirmation of the Holy Trinity, respect for Scripture, and expectation of a future new creation. However loathe they may be to recognize it, mainline attempts to critique the positions of the right wing have to be understood as, in some sense, intramural conflicts. But mainline Protestants are reluctant to conduct theological debates in public, and particularly do not want to contribute to the general impression that people with faith convictions of whatever sort are likely to be disagreeable, in every sense of the word. They are constrained by their desire not to be, or even appear to be, unloving, unchristian.

In the meantime, the newly energized skeptics are not held back by any worry about restraining their critique of aggressive evangelicalism. Their critique, supported by the New Atheists,[1] is easily enough a full-on attack against faith itself, and particularly Christian faith, with no exceptions made for the mainline.

Mainline Protestants, whose critiques have been mostly low-key and in-house, note that, to a degree, the skeptics make more headway than the

---

1. Particularly, Sam Harris, Richard Dawkins, Daniel Dennett, and Christopher Hitchens.

6

mainliners do in pushing back against evangelical attempts to seize control of the public spaces. Both skeptics and ecumenical Protestants share an appreciation for science, an opposition to anti-intellectualism, and a greater openness to much of the social change that has emerged in the past few decades. It is not surprising, then, that mainliners who feel crowded and even bullied by extremists who are fellow Christians might begin to see the skeptics as friendly allies.

Of course, there has been no declaration of an alliance between religious skeptics and mainline Protestants. The skeptics have no interest in the mainliners and no particular need for them unless it should be in some specific skirmish that brings them together on the same side. Nevertheless, there is something to the old adage, "The enemy of my enemy is my friend." "Enemy" is an overstatement, even a misstatement in the case of the mainline vs. aggressive evangelicalism, but the point is clear enough. When mainliners find themselves in debt to the skeptics for holding at bay extremist forms of Christianity, the skeptics seem to be the friendlier party. A practical consequence is that mainline Protestants often find it tempting to go easy on those parts of their message that might seem to mark them as being on the same side as theological/political evangelicalism, or might cause them to alienate skeptically inclined persons in their own pews.

Doctrine/Theology: Irrelevant?

Where this muting of specifically Christian doctrine occurs, not many have set out to do it consciously or deliberately, as though it were a carefully thought out strategy. It is more likely to develop unconsciously, unintentionally, the product not of strategizing but of a kind of intuitive sense of how to appeal to congregations who may have been made suspicious of God-talk. Or, at least, made suspicious of Jesus-talk. Suspicious because mainliners have recoiled from the easy way aggressively militant Christians have used God-talk and Jesus-talk as though they had a direct and unambiguous line of communication with the divine. "God sent this hurricane upon these people because . . ." or "God caused this person to be elected to office because . . ." Or, "Jesus told me to . . ." No discussion. No debate. No questions; no modest hesitation or mutual consultation; just direct and unambiguous communication, accessible only to those who are willing to accept the premise that God works that way, at least with those whom God favors.

Absorbing by osmosis a sense of which direction mainline church members may be leaning, it becomes easy and natural for those who preach or teach to feel it might be prudent to go easy on addressing basic issues of a theological nature. Without rejecting specifically Christian doctrine, it is possible, perhaps unconsciously, to begin to lean ever so carefully toward favoring teaching and preaching about issues of personal or social morality. In other words, maybe lifting up the teachings of Jesus, but not so much the identity or unique authority of the person of Jesus. After all, aren't the people in the pews likely to be uninterested in theology, even wary of it? Maybe even to identify it with the aggressively evangelical? Or to recoil from classic doctrinal affirmations that have become the targets of anti-theological scorn fashionable in some circles? When such presumptions prevail, theologizing can become muted; moralizing increases proportionately.

However, in my experience, church people in the pews bring with them a whole host of theological questions, whether recognized as such or not. And, given an opening, they are eager to explore them. These theological questions may very well be interwoven with questions of morality or the interpretation of social issues. But even though the skeptics' arguments may trouble church members or even influence their thinking, many church folk are still willing to enter into a hopeful and expectant conversation with the faith of the church. In my estimation, the best response to aggressive forms of Christian imperialistic ambitions, and to aggressive skepticism as well, can be discovered in the richness of classic Christian thought and practice. In other words, the strategy should not be to go to war with either of the extreme parties, but to pursue another way by investigating more deeply the resources that have been available to us all along: thoughtful attention to Scripture and the ages-long internal theological conversation of the church.

Rediscovering the Energy of the Gospel Always Begins with Sources

Ours would not be the first era in which confusing times have led us to dig more deeply into beginnings—revisiting basic sources of our faith. Throughout history, many such moments have confronted Christians. The sources are at least these:

- the Bible, both testaments;

- the sacraments;

- the gospel as it has been preached and taught with some recognizable consistency;

- the ecumenical creeds (Apostles' and Nicene, in particular);

- and we must not leave out the church itself, the assembly of those for whom Jesus Christ is Lord.

They are the identity markers that describe the community that has, over two millennia, established a broad but authoritative consensus about the substance of the Christian faith. It is from within that consensus that the ecumenical community's conversations and debates find their bearings. From those touchstones we can explore the various dimensions of faith, not just ways of thinking about it, but also ways of embodying it, both individually and corporately. Engaging the sources, we will meet prophets, but also apostles. We will meet those for whom faith seems to have come naturally, but also those who have had to struggle mightily to hold on to it.

When the moment requires a resolve to refresh our faith, we go back in order to go forward. We return to the sources to reexamine and re-experience them, bringing with us our own contemporary discoveries, issues, concerns, conflicts, and limitations. Integrity and faithfulness require that renewal of faith necessarily begin with the sources, from which we listen together with reverent attention, hoping to hear, together, a word from the Lord of the church.

I have been writing this book in my head for several years, based on unsystematic but engaged observation through several lenses available to me. It is in some ways a continuation of a project of reflection on our present situation that began with my book *Finding Our Balance: Repositioning Mainstream Protestantism*, but this time focused more specifically on the phenomenon of faith itself.

I have long been a participant/observer in the church. An observer, because my experience has offered me a panoramic view of the faith, life, and worship of the church, including the ways in which they are manifest in the local congregation. For most of my working life, my line of sight was from behind the pulpit. For some years, it was from behind the lectern in a seminary classroom. In the most recent, overlapping years, my perspective has been formed from the vantage point of various pews, some consistently, others occasional.

My perspective is that of a student of liturgics with a deep interest in preaching, and also from experience as a pastor committed to teaching, mentoring, and lifelong learning. But not only am I an observer, I am a participant as well, because the church's faith, its teaching, service, preaching, sacraments, praise and prayer matter to me deeply on a personal level. So I write for the sake of all sorts of church people, with a continuing commitment to the local church in particular fueling my effort. It is in the worshiping congregation where the Bible most reliably finds its audience.

The primary context for engaging the Bible is in an assembly for prayer and praise, ideally juxtaposed to a (sacramental) meal. In his teaching and writing, Gordon Lathrop has pointed this out, and the liturgist or preacher may actually recognize the truth of it intuitively.[2] Certainly it has been my experience, if only because liturgical language—the language of worship—is profoundly indebted to biblical language, and so it is inseparable from the faith embodied in it. The Bible was not formed with private study in mind, whether by individual readers or specialized students, but rather intended to be read aloud in assemblies of the faithful. "The "*plain* sense [of it] is often already, *from the beginning*, a figurative or poetic or doxological sense!"[3] And it is precisely this figurative, poetic, or doxological sense that is communicated most naturally when we are "lost in wonder, love, and praise."[4] On the other hand, when we read this magnificent language as though it were written for a classroom, we are at risk of missing the point. To forget or lose track of the essential context of the worshiping community invites a distorted reading, whether from the fundamentalist's side or the skeptic's.

I write as one who loves the Bible, with which I have been fortunate enough as a preacher to become engaged weekly in the preparation of sermons. I reflect as one who loves the creeds, the distillation of the Christian proclamation; and one who cherishes the sacraments that, along with preaching, become meeting places with the God who can never be possessed, but nevertheless somehow known. I write as a Trinitarian, believing with the great tradition that the only God of whom Christians dare attempt to speak is the God revealed to us in Christ as Father, Son, and Holy Spirit. And I write as one who believes this question is an urgent one: Is it still possible to have faith in God when so many who claim faith do it aggressively,

2. See, for example, Lathrop, *Four Gospels on Sunday*.

3. Lathrop, in a private communication with the author.

4. Charles Wesley, "Love Divine."

immodestly, and with apparently little respect for those who do not share it?

Atheists by Thursday?

Faith is, in some sense, always a mystery. Some people have it, some don't, and it is not at all apparent why one does or does not. At the same time, there are in between places, when a person is unsure whether she has faith, or even wants to have it. This is where a lot of people find themselves, or would recognize themselves if they were still likely to be involved in late-night, free-ranging conversations covering a wide swath of questions, concerns, and experimental commitments. This book is meant to be a contribution to discussions real and hypothetical having to do with the phenomenon of faith.

Pastor Ron Luckey preached a sermon to his Lutheran congregation in which he said something like, "I'm a believer on Sunday, but nearly an atheist by Thursday." Perhaps for some a shocking statement, but most of the listening congregation understood him without any requirement of an explanation. This is, for a fact, the experience of many of us. We gather with the congregation on Sunday, and faith feels relatively secure. However subtly, God makes the divine presence known, sufficiently at least to strengthen our trust, our confidence, and reenergize our hope. But when we leave the assembly, we are likely to be on our own. We reenter a world that has been demystified, as though everything real in the universe or beyond it could be summed up by referring to a list of mechanical causes and effects, some identifiable, some yet to be decoded. In ordinary conversation, apart from curses, we are not likely to hear God mentioned, or Christ. It is as though, whatever one's personal faith, for all practical purposes we live in a godless universe. In most cases, our weekday journey meets with nothing more threatening than indifference: who cares? God-talk, church-talk is reserved for a small slice of a one-seventh slice of the week, if that. A hobby, if you like, for those so inclined. Indifference fills all the space available, and faith is likely to find itself disabled, irrelevant, pushed off to a private corner. In other cases, we encounter not indifference, but something between suspicion and scorn for a faith presumed to be superstition—a consolation for the weak, a force to narrow the mind, a cold leftover from the past. By Thursday, we have been worn down.

The more we are aware of and sensitive to theological/ideological fundamentalisms, the more appealing a blissful state of indifference becomes. It does not take much exposure to find oneself sufficiently repelled as to want to distance ourselves as decisively as possible, to shake the dust off our feet, to stalk off and leave it all to the extremists who seem to have kidnapped the God we thought we knew. It would not be so hard, by Thursday, to forsake the faith entirely, the censors' cranky Jesus who is big on disapproval; the ungenerous Jesus of the radio preachers, who seems altogether unlike the Jesus to whom we were introduced in our Bible and our hymnal.

When we find ourselves offended by the easy Jesus-talk of many evangelical preachers and talk-show hosts and their constituents, there comes a moment of irritation at which we wonder whether we are able to talk about him at all. We are not familiar with the mostly ticked-off Jesus, the finger-pointing Jesus, the Jesus who is apparently committed above all else to free markets and American exceptionalism, the one who favors some kinds of people over the other kinds (and you know who they are). But ecumenically minded Christians cannot afford to hand Jesus over to those who take for granted that he supports an uncritically presumed us-against-them agenda. It is the Jesus of the gospel and the church catholic and reforming who challenges both our opponents' prejudices and our own, and whose life, death, and resurrection unfold for us promises that are reliable, capable of creating life out of death, and chasing fear away.

Pastor Luckey's statement about faith barely surviving the various weekday challenges was intended to remind his congregation of the fact that faith, while not necessarily fragile, is strengthened where it finds support. That support no longer comes from the general approval of the larger culture. It may come from various personal sources here and there, but the chief means of support is the church itself. Christianity is a faith in which assembling together on a regular basis is part of the very substance of who we are. Like the twelve disciples whom Jesus gathered, we are not making this journey by ourselves. We may meet zombies or demons along the way, and we shall certainly meet all sorts of seductions and misdirection, but we are not traveling alone. It is not even possible to comprehend the meaning of the gospel apart from the disciplines, challenges, difficulties, and support that comes with being part of what the apostle called the "body of Christ" (e.g., 1 Cor 12:27).

What Is Faith, Anyway?

We are not the first generation to have experienced the need for support when the prevailing winds have been against us. Certainly the first Christians faced a much more difficult environment than we do. After all, in the U. S. there is, in fact, no "war on Christmas." We are not persecuted, we are not victims, and no one is trying to stop us from going to church or from expressing our faith. Feeling, to some extent at least, at odds with the prevailing culture has been the norm for many in the more than two millennia of Christian history, beginning with the apostolic age itself. Nevertheless, our current experience reflects a cultural change to which we are not accustomed. It feels as though the landmarks have been moved and we find ourselves lost, not sure where we are when it comes to matters of faith. Even when our own faith is strong, we are uneasy at the prospect of having to defend it, either to a skeptic or to ourselves. When we try to explain it, we cannot help being very much aware that our explanations might not actually explain anything to our skeptical conversation partners, or even that part of ourselves that craves to know it all, uneasy with mystery.

I began this writing to organize my own thoughts. The eight chapters represent several approaches to the question suggested in the title of the book. They may be read in any order. It will be clear enough that I believe that faith is misunderstood if it is imagined to be only an intellectual decision. While faith can be expressed intellectually, and is intellectually defensible, it is a more complex phenomenon than one that involves only doing some research and settling on an opinion. Faith is not easily explained in scientific terms. To begin to understand what faith is requires being open to a measure of subtlety that is not readily laid down in a tightly reasoned argument. My purpose is to explore some of the subtleties.

Martin Luther is supposed to have said that human beings cannot even think without images. In other words, the reality represented in language is visualized internally in images fashioned in the mind—imagination. Imagination is required to recall things now past, or to anticipate the future. When someone we love lives far away, or has died, we hold in our minds an image of them. When we consider our own path, we imagine various possible scenarios unfolding. To think of a proton or a bacterium, it is necessary to form some tentative image in our minds of what such a thing might be like. Our ability to imagine—i.e., to form mental images— is essential whenever we have to ponder anyone or anything that is not directly in front of us, and that certainly applies to thinking about God, whether as Creator, or as incarnate in Jesus of Nazareth, or as Holy Spirit. The language of the Bible, or of the worshiping church, and even of formal theology is language that evokes images. We are far more dependent on a capacity for image making than we might think, even in matters of science as well as in matters of faith.

The theme of imagination will be addressed directly and again occasionally throughout the book, as will the theme of "knowing." Our era is one in which appreciation for science rises so high in the hierarchy of values that it seems as though nothing important can be "known" except by the use of the scientific method. And yet, for tens of thousands of years people have known things about the world, their neighbors, and themselves without consciously or unconsciously making use of a scientific method. And it can be argued that they have also known some things of an eternal nature without the help of that method. The book will talk about various ways of "knowing," without claiming infallibility for any of them, and will make a case that it is possible, apart from the scientific method, to know some things, and even some things of great importance.

The book will directly address the question of faith: what is it? How does one acquire it? And how does one hold on to it in the face of challenges? Faith can be described as an ongoing process of responding to God reaching out to us. Responding involves, insofar as it can be described at all, as personal engagement of a kind that is holistic—body, mind, and spirit. Responding to God's initiative involves, so far as we can find words for it, a coordination of imagination, sensing, emotional intelligence, and intuition, accompanied by observation and informed reasoning. Faith is served by questioning and being questioned, doubt playing a role in the process. To sustain faith beyond Thursdays, we look for support from a community that embodies something properly named as "the faith of the church." How is faith formed in us by Christian practices, for example, as well as Christian thought? Particularly, how do the practices of worship and discipleship inform and direct our love toward the appropriate objects of our love?

The intention of the book is to offer a hand up to those who find themselves negotiating challenges to faith every day. The challenges come particularly, in our era, from two broadly defined parties, each of whom claims to be dealing in absolute certainties. One of those parties is composed of the anxious and defensive theological/ideological evangelicals and their parallels in other faiths, and the other is the diverse party of determined atheists and casual skeptics. These are not the only options.

An option for which I contend is the classic faith of the ecumenical church: catholic, evangelical in the original and non-partisan sense, and re-forming. This rich tradition offers the best response to the equally distressing certainty of the two parties that presently claim most public attention. This is not a call to hand-to-hand combat or to a raucous debate, but a call to pause, take a deep breath, and be strengthened by the confidence that a loving and gracious God has not ceased to speak or to gather and sustain a people even when the times are confusing.

1

Imagination

We must be willing to imagine the world that Scripture imagines, and by so doing to find in our empirical world the basis for such imagination.

— LUKE TIMOTHY JOHNSON[1]

Language Problems

THINKING ABOUT CHRISTIAN FAITH of the sort that is resilient enough to resist the appeals of political/ideological evangelicalism on the one hand, or skepticism on the other, will likely require us to shift gears. When we hear the word "faith," we are likely to think of it, rather too simply, as "belief." In other words, to think of it as basically an intellectual transaction. Thinking more deeply about the phenomenon of faith requires an exercise that is and is not similar to what has traditionally been labeled as "apologetics." Apologetics refers to the formation of rational arguments to support Christian faith. Karl Barth, a theologian whom I much admire, did not believe that it was possible to make Christians by way of reasonable arguments. He was right, I believe, in the sense that to frame the gospel in the kind of language that suits what passes for scientific, analytic reasoning is and ever must be an alien language as far as faith formation is concerned.

1. Johnson, *Revelatory Body*, 75.

While it may persuade the mind, it cannot be expected to affect heart/soul/spirit, which, alongside the mind, is essential for faith.

However, rational arguments may be helpful in the case of those who already experience faith, whether to a greater or lesser degree, or find themselves open to it. Such persons may find reassurance in organized ways of thinking that demonstrate that, while not something one is argued into, faith is nevertheless conceptually reasonable. A rational argument may include describing human capacities for engaging reality in ways that do not rely on intellectualizing alone. The intention of using reasoning in this way is not to persuade unbelieving people into becoming believers. Rather, it aims to describe and commend to people inclined toward faith a respect for the non-cognitive experiences that draw them towards it. Such reasoning is useful as a means of supporting church people who encounter every day a dismissive attitude toward faith, as though it should be obvious that no reasonable or scientifically inclined person could ever take faith seriously.

An article in a Sunday *New York Times* caught my attention by its title: "Don't Believe in God? Maybe You'll Try U.F.O.s." The writer cited the by-now familiar statistics about the decline of religious affiliation and observance in the U.S. Nevertheless, he points out that turning away from traditional faiths has not put to an end the search for meaning of some kind.

> People who do not frequently attend church are twice as likely to believe in ghosts as those who are regular churchgoers. The less religious people are, the more likely they are to endorse empirically unsupported ideas about U.F.O.s, intelligent aliens monitoring the lives of humans and related conspiracies about a government cover-up of these phenomena.[2]

At least some of those who have turned away from faith appear to see those who believe in the God of the Bible as simple-minded, self-serving, and credulous. On the other hand, it might be the case that it is the unbeliever lacking imagination, or that the unbeliever's imagination has been narrowed by a dominant culture that bends the knee to "scientism." "Scientism" is to be distinguished from science. Scientism is a distorted view of the scientific enterprise as seen by non-scientists. It grants too much authority to those who would flatten out everything, reducing the intricate macro- and micro-complexities of a multi-faceted reality to what can be empirically detected, measured, and counted. Certainly many will find it a

2. Routledge, "Try U.F.O.s." *New York Times*, July 21, 2017.

stretch to believe in a Creator God who became incarnate in Christ crucified and risen, and whose ultimate purpose is to fashion a new creation.
But, "because beliefs about U.F.O.s and aliens do not explicitly invoke the
supernatural and are couched in scientific and technological jargon," they
give the appearance of a respectable credibility.

The Necessity of Imagination

The word "imagination" has at least two meanings. One, perhaps the most
common, is that to imagine something is the same as just making it up. It
is a fantasy, a delusion. The other meaning is to understand the capacity to
imagine as an ability to perceive more deeply—to "see" in one's mind what
is not readily at hand to be tested for, measured or counted, for example.
Indeed, even for the practice of science, imagination is a basic requirement.
Atoms had to be imagined before their existence could be verified by physical and mathematical measurements. To conceive of the "speed of light"
required the ability to imagine that light is actually in motion in space.
Without the capacity for imagination, it is doubtful that it would have been
discovered that the world is round and that there are continents on the far
side of what had seemed an unending sea.

To try to discern meaning of any kind, scientific or not, requires
imagination. The hard-nosed realist with no use for faith "sees" the world
and the universe in a certain way with the help of habits of imagination
vouched for by similar-thinking peers. To discern a big picture—one as big
as the horizons of faith—is a challenge. Our planet is one among many. The
universe is vast. The solar system is estimated to be about five billion years
old, and the age of the universe is estimated to be about three times that.
We have imagined and then verified physical laws and their relation to each
other. Patterns in the world and in the universe have been made manifest,
some easily observable and some yet to be identified. It is possible to trace
back from an effect to its cause. But what is not available to scientific test
or discernment is whether what we can see or measure is all there is, or
whether any of it *means* anything.

Is there any intentionality in the universe or behind it or beyond it?
Any purpose, any destination, either for the universe itself or for humanity
as a whole, or for me? To think or speak of *meaning* in that broad, yet personally urgent sense requires the ability to imagine what is not otherwise

susceptible to investigation. To imagine in faith is to be able to imagine the world differently from other, conventional ways it's possible to imagine it.

When the church speaks about a Creator God whose character and disposition are known to us not by our own investigatory skills but by God's own self-revealing, it is easy to judge that such talk is all imaginary, in the sense of making things up, fantasy, delusion. After all, Sigmund Freud and others have made a judgment that religious faith is a fantasy that served some evolutionary purpose in the history of human development—maybe reassurance, maybe a summons to courage. But, a critique of Freud's opinion might be to argue that if there is in human nature a rudimentary sense of the divine, it may just as easily be that it is God who has embedded that sense in us, making instrumental use of evolutionary processes. Not fantasy, but the foundation for an intuitive sense that life does have meaning, and that the search for it is not fruitless, and that the search itself is part of what life means.

God of the Gaps

In any case, when the church refers to God, it is not as though God is an impersonal force, even an ultimate force that is part of the structured universe. God is not like a super-nova or a black hole or a neutron or quark that is subject to scientific investigation. By definition, a Creator of all things is other than all things. And not being a phenomenon within the universe, it is not possible to devise tests that would determine whether God is, or is not.

And yet, it is a common presumption in our culture that because science is gradually advancing, it will sooner or later deliver a conclusive answer about God. Gaps in our knowledge used to be filled rather too easily by the suggestion that God was to be found in the gaps for which we had as yet no explanation. So, an eclipse of the sun, an earthquake, or a tsunami, otherwise puzzling, might be interpreted as a sign from God. One could speculate about the meaning of such signs. Punishment for sins? (Usually, someone else's!) A powerful statement about who is in charge here? A warning shot across the bow?

As science has advanced, we have discovered the causes of unusual phenomena or occurrences for which there had earlier been no causes that we could discern. To make sense of such phenomena it is no longer necessary to plug our gaps in knowledge by hauling in God to serve as an all-purpose explanation. Should the day come when all the puzzling phenomena shall have been researched and explained, it is easy to presume that there will be no room for any God. No gaps; no need for God.

It is certainly true that under those circumstances there would no longer be need for arguing God's reality on the basis of something missing in our scientific knowledge. But it is not true that science will be able sooner or later to produce a definitive conclusion about God. Science may, conceivably, reach a point of being able to explain all the processes of the universe and describe exhaustively how it came to be or perhaps always has been. But the basic definition of a Creator God is of one who must be imagined to be over and above, not containable within the created world, not available for scientific authentication or, for that matter, to be denied conclusively. That is not to say that individual scientists will not form their own opinions about God should they choose to, not to mention non-scientists who often grant to science greater powers than most scientists do. But their opinions are formed in the same ways as anyone else's. In other words, the personal views of scientists and science aficionados in reference to God will not be privileged or authoritative, whether scientifically or theologically.

To say anything at all about God—whatever that little three-letter word means—requires imagination. Of course, most of us are quite able to imagine all sorts of gods, in the sense of constructing fantasies. The Reformer John Calvin charged that the human mind is a virtual factory for the manufacture of idols—i.e., false gods. But the other sort of imagination—discerning a reality that cannot be measured or counted or observed or tested for—is essential if it is possible at all to "see" what cannot be observed or proved. Should some sense of the divine have been genetically seeded in human beings by means of the very evolutionary processes involved in our formation, it could as easily be true that God has given us the gift of imagination that we might somehow come to perceive the giver of the gift.

Of course, while the gift of imagination may be a clue to help us to recognize our Creator, to say anything more about this God it is necessary to resort to the intellectual tools available to us within the experiential and comprehensible framework of a three-dimensional world. Which is to say, the true God, the only one that matters, is bigger than the load-bearing capacity of our human instruments. Our imagination (i.e., our images) will never be big enough for us to "see" God directly. To "see" at all we must make use of knowledgeable intuition, expressing it indirectly in language and images that are different from language used for objective descriptions.

Meaning?

What does any of this have to do with the current status of Christian faith in a society in which it no longer carries the authority that it once did? For one thing, it is necessary to remind ourselves that human beings have not evolved beyond their basic, necessary hunger and thirst for meaning. They will seek it out, looking for it carefully or carelessly, appropriately and inappropriately. Maybe some will decide that *meaning* in the broadest sense is just too big a challenge, so they will choose to find it within smaller, more manageable circles: family, work, politics, mathematics, philosophy, physics, collections of experiences (the bucket list), etc. "Meaning" is more easily discoverable within the parameters of discrete areas of interest bounded by three-dimensional space and time than is the search for ultimate meaning. Some may be quite satisfied with that—or at least claim to be.

Others, in search of the big picture, will find satisfaction in directing their exploration to U.F.O.s, ghosts, psychic phenomena, reincarnation (respectable in Buddhism or Hinduism, but the equivalent, in those faiths, of hell), or other kinds of what seem to be science-like theories or paranormal beliefs. And, of course, in "scientism"—not science, which is, in its own way, comparatively modest in its claims—the conviction that eventually science can and will reveal to us every hidden meaning if only we surrender all authority to it.

Today it is common for persons in authority—celebrities, musicians, artists, novelists, academics, CEOs, professionals of all sorts—to explain in interviews that they were raised Catholic or Baptist or Presbyterian or Jewish, but those connections are past tense. Equally common is the declaration by high-profile persons that they are "not religious," "spiritual, but not religious," atheist or agnostic. As far as the media are concerned—including, of course, social networks and online resources of every kind—there is likely to be very little exposure to God-talk. When there is, it is likely to run the gamut from a vastly over-confident fundamentalism to a similarly over-confident skepticism. In both cases, examples of limitations generated by an inability to perceive the necessarily subtle ways that language must be deployed to speak of things that are real though not objectively verifiable.

Conversion of the Imagination

It appears that "meaning," when corralled into relatively smaller parameters, does not necessarily provide much satisfaction. Those who experience an itch to ponder the big picture, even if they are unable to identify and label what that itch is, are likely to be disappointed with, say, ecclesiastical coaching on how to deal with stress or ringing the changes on how to effect social transformations. When a church becomes too shy to risk the language necessary for imagining the big picture, some adherents will accommodate themselves to a little picture, while others will sink into indifference or drift away. A few will turn to a fascination with visiting aliens or *Feng Shui*, or whatever satisfies a transcendent need while looking vaguely science-like, thus passing for something intellectually respectable.

The church has answered a vocation to represent big picture "meaning," anchored in a particular set of narratives.[3] To retreat from that properly focused task, even when contemporary conditions may not seem to be in our favor, will not prove to be an effective long-term strategy. To live up to our calling, even under optimal circumstances, is a challenge, but it is a challenge that cannot be ducked without unacceptable sacrifices. It is simply unacceptable that we should turn Jesus Christ over to a relatively small part of the Christian church, one that is characterized by what seems to be an ungenerous view of the God to whom the great church has testified for two millennia.

Richard Hays describes how the apostle Paul called for "his readers and hearers to a *conversion of the imagination*."[4] Without imagination, we are certain to misunderstand the gospel, either taking it to be a kind of carrot-and-stick affair meant to keep us in line, or a comforting fantasy for those for whom almost any fantasy would do if it promises to provide a shield from the emptiness that may seem to be all there is. But faith is not about hiding from reality or trying to pretty it up just to keep ourselves from despair. It is to embrace God's own initiative in the gospel, calling us to imagine the world as it could be, taking seriously the biblical vision of a new creation in Christ, and looking in hopeful expectation to the Creator who is not finished creating.

---

3. Postmodern philosophy is suspicious of so-called "meta-narratives," and certainly there is no big-picture narrative likely to achieve consensus in a whole culture. But that suspicion does not mean that there is no big picture.

4. Hays, *Conversion of the Imagination*, 5.

Imagining the Suppleness of Language

A "conversion of the imagination" consistent with the gospel requires the ability to imagine God, who can never be directly and entirely conceptualized, about whom our words must always be stumbling. It requires finding language that projects God's reality while not boxing God in. It requires being able to imagine, for example, resurrection—not the resuscitation of a corpse or changing into a ghost—and to discern in Christ's resurrection how vulnerability and vindication may paradoxically be wrapped together. It requires perceiving in his resurrection a promise about the ultimate and universal future—not just one's own ultimate future.

Even those many church members who know that a literal interpretation of the Bible is not always the best one don't always know where to go from there. Most mainline congregations have grasped by now that not every biblical text is appropriately read literally. They understand that the Bible often uses metaphorical language. However, the problem is that in our society, "metaphor" is easily dismissed: "It's *only* a metaphor!" In other words, it is not to be taken as seriously as information-giving, analytic language. So, one either passes over the metaphor as though it is merely a literary ornament to be noticed, admired, and laid aside, or tries to translate it into textbook language that is bound to fall flat because the power of the language is in the metaphor itself.

When the metaphor is not taken seriously, and the attempt is made to translate it into a language that misses the multivalent nuance of the metaphor, the interpretation of a biblical text will often seem arbitrary or insignificant. It is easy enough to judge an interpretation as though it were entirely subjective, anchored nowhere in particular, and, therefore, exerting no particular claim on us. Scholars, on the other hand, may debate the original meaning of a text, but they know that the text cannot be made to say just anything at all. The very richness of such texts is related to the fact that we can hear the same voice speaking in them with an originally time-contextual message that nevertheless speaks consistently to other and newer times and contexts when we listen with the help of the imagination. To encounter a metaphor genuinely requires permitting oneself to engage the capacity to imagine. That is, to be able to "see" the images sparked by a metaphor, as well as by the tensions rising from several metaphors set side by side. Such images are likely to prove relevant in more than one era.

Ancient Texts for the Twenty-first Century

A novelist is invited to meet with a group of her readers. While she mostly listens, they engage with each other in an earnest discussion of her novel: its themes, sub-texts, and images they have caught in their process of interacting with it. She nods from time to time, and may affirm something small or large she had intended in her writing that they have, happily, noticed. But sometimes, she is taken by surprise. She had not meant to say something they are sure they had discovered in her novel; but, as she reflects, she has to admit that what they have perceived to be there is, in fact, there. At some points, the novel has provided a vessel for some idea, image, or concern to break through even before she had organized her thought about it or even recognized its existence. The group, reflecting together, has brought to the novel from their varied experiences a way of "hearing" or "seeing" that accurately recognizes something of which their creator had not been entirely conscious at the moment of writing.

The novelist's reading of—what shall we say? Human experience? The tensions at work in society? The paradox of loving and loathing coexisting in the same persons, family, community? Her imagination was at work to fashion a story, the details of which she was piecing together in her own mind, partly deliberately and partly unconsciously, working with whatever materials that had been impressed upon her in the course of living. The resulting story, an artistic creation, she had fashioned as a way of telling the truth. Her imagination was not divorced from reality, but engaged with the real, whether consciously perceived or not, and her writing enables the unnoticed to be noticed and pondered.

The kind of imagination that enables hearing and seeing something not perceived on the surface is not free-floating. In the case of the novel, it is anchored in experience, including a writer's experience even when it has not always been consciously registered, at least in an organized way; but also in the receiving experience of the readers. In the case of the Christian faith, theological imagination is anchored in the arc of the narrative lines of the Bible and in the ongoing tradition—i.e., the persistent conversation of the teaching church, rooted in Scripture, as well as faith's interactions with the broader culture and responses to expansions in general knowledge over time. And, also, as in the case of the novel, anchored in the receiving experience of readers both ancient and contemporary.

The Bible: A Textbook about God?

It is a curious thing that people who are not fundamentalists are usually able to recognize figures of speech, metaphors, and poetic representations when they encounter them in a novel, a play, a film, or a popular song. It is by no means unknown that language can work differently in various settings. Language is, after all, a tool—an instrument capable of communicating in more than one way. And yet, even non-fundamentalist Christians often bring to the Bible the expectation that since it is a "holy book," it should be read as though it were a textbook about God and holy things. As though it should be read with the same eyes we bring to a user's manual or to printed directions about how to find the nearest interstate highway. Maybe to approach the Bible as we might indifferently scan the lyrics of a song, but without hearing or feeling the music.

But the Bible is not a textbook and does not normally deal with theological questions systematically. Rather, it engages theological questions narratively, telling stories and evoking images that often communicate subtly and indirectly. Biblical literalists and skeptics may find themselves reading Scripture in similar ways. Are there biblical texts that speak of God's wrath? Of having a tantrum? Of God repenting, having a change of heart? Are there texts that imply that God can be located somewhere, in a "place" called heaven? The fundamentalist may feel pressed to defend such linguistic representations as though they come straight from God and must be taken as direct representations of reality. The skeptic may feel that they illustrate how childish or inconsequential the Bible is. In either case, both fundamentalist and skeptic have turned off their normally available capacity to recognize the variety of supple and nuanced ways that language may be used to communicate something that is different from and more than a piece of objective information.

One might wish that it were possible to speak about God in straightforward, journalistic language. However, there is no straightforward language available to us when it comes to God, who is not a sort of Extra Big human being whom we might be able to predict or second-guess. To speak of God it is necessary to use language and images that only serve adequately as vessels for communication so long as communication is not limited to intellectual representations alone.

Biblical writing, and also theological language and the language of worship make use of anthropomorphisms. In other words, we speak of God as though God were one of us. Is God angry? Have tantrums? Whatever the original writer may have thought, that anthropomorphic language is consistent in pointing to the fact that, were God a human being, God would have plenty of reason to be entitled to be dismayed, and to consider indulging an understandable impulse to give it to us with both barrels. Does God "repent"? Experience a changed mind? Or is that an indirect way of pointing to God's character as morally and ethically serious, but also merciful and forgiving? John Calvin, one of the sixteenth-century Reformers, suggested that such language is, basically, baby talk. It is language that can serve well enough to reveal God's character and disposition in a fashion comprehensible to mortal beings with all our limitations.

The use of anthropomorphisms evokes the conviction that God, who is more than a "person," is nevertheless at least "personal"—not indifferent to us, but reaching out in love. That "love" is other than, different from, and greater than human love, but can nevertheless be identified faithfully enough with that simple word. To speak of God as God alone knows the divine self is impossible for mortals.

Not Textbook, but Meeting Place

From the Christian point of view, the Bible is to be held in respect and reverence because in it and through it we have experienced a kind of engagement with the holy God. (An engagement that can occur even without explanations about the various uses of language!) The Bible is, as we tend to perceive it, a human artifact, a product of human beings who used language in a variety of modes to hand on to others their own and their community's experience of God's self-communication, filtered through several cultures and histories, and often most powerfully expressed not in analytic language but in images.

In a sermon, the Rev. David H. C. Read reflected on his own growth in coming to understand that the Bible ought not be understood as a textbook, competing, for example, with the scientific understanding of evolution. He told his congregation that

> It was an immense relief when it dawned on me that I was comparing, not just apples and oranges, but the apple as the scientist analyses it and the apple as seen by the artist in a radiant still life.[5]

5. Read, *Preacher*, 118.

From the point of view of faith, we believe we can discern the work of the Holy Spirit in the Bible's creation and in its reception. It is not a direct transcription of speech from God to humankind, but a vehicle, an artistic creation from many hands, by which the holy One has chosen to engage with us. "Engage" is a key word. The Bible is reduced when we think of it as a list of ideas, or impersonal history, or explanations to be learned, or a set of doctrines to be mastered, as though our engagement with it were only by means of the intellect. It is, rather, a place of meeting—only rarely like being thunderstruck—more often subtle, unfolding more slowly than we might prefer. We find ourselves in Scripture; the world and its people will be found in it; and God is in it. It is a meeting place. The Bible is, in a sense, to be experienced. No argument about its authority is sufficient to compensate when we are unable to give ourselves permission to trust that experience.

A sermon is, in a sense, also a meeting place. When the sermon engages the preacher, the listeners, and the biblical text in its larger context, without forgetting the God who is in and behind it, the sermon becomes a holistic experience. At least for a moment or two, it may become an engagement with God evoking a response in heart, mind, and soul.

Bible and sermon, in quite different ways, open up the "big picture" that human beings long to glimpse. We are a questioning people, and in both Bible and sermon answers may emerge and be discernible. They are set within the framework of an even broader Christian tradition that is not without abundant intellectual resources. But the Bible and the sermon, when the connection is made with listeners, also question us, and the questions require of us an answer. Whom or what do we love most? How do our various loves shape our lives both in close quarters and in the larger society? Where and when might love be misdirected? Where have we perhaps been deceived? Or deceived ourselves? How should our loves be shaped? How do we follow through on them with something like consistency? Are we able, if only for a moment, to imagine what our loving would look like if we should embrace and prove sensitive to the judgment and the mercy of the God of the big picture? Can we imagine a world healed, reconciled, where love and justice prevail? To experience faith requires learning to permit oneself to trust the eye-opening power of imagination.

2

Knowing

For we know only in part, and we prophesy only in part;
but when the complete comes, the partial will come to an end.

— ROMANS 13:9-10

The Language of the Scientific Method

THE ENLIGHTENMENT, OR AGE of Reason, came to full flower in the eighteenth century and has been exerting its influence ever since. It was a major watershed in human history, an attempt to overcome lingering superstition and irrational prejudices that feed ignorance and support conflict. It was a movement to achieve rational goals by the use of pure reason. As such, it was an important and necessary evolutionary moment in the history of human thought, and continues to contribute to the unmasking of the stubbornly irrational. A problem, however, is that there really is no such thing as "pure reason." Reason is never entirely pure; i.e., neutral. Reason is not wholly independent of the contexts in which and for which it is being exercised. The long-lasting Enlightenment era seems to have reached a point at which some weaknesses have become more evident. We are straining toward something new that will incorporate the best of what Enlightenment devotion to reason has to offer while mending some of its blind spots.

In the era of quantum physics, the by-now centuries-old Enlightenment era may be morphing into a different version of itself. Along the way, Enlightenment presuppositions have inadvertently contributed to a narrowing of the way we permit ourselves to engage with the world. Yes, in its time it had the opposite effect. Its commitment to rational thought first broadened our engagement with the world by suppressing superstition and honoring empirical, critical, and analytic ways of learning. For that gift, we should be grateful. But, as is often the case in many realms of life, what began as broadening had unintended consequences, becoming, sooner or later, a narrowing.

The narrowing consists of shutting down respect for our inborn capacity for engaging the world holistically, for taking seriously the precognitive ways that contribute to healthy and realistic access to the whole of our environment, including the parts of it not expressible in words. We became suspicious of a whole category of experience that might accurately be described as one way of "knowing." The resulting over-valuation of rational detachment has contributed to religious skepticism, on the one hand, as precognitive ways of knowing have been devalued; and to fundamentalisms on the other.

Fundamentalism is a defensive means of bracing itself against a narrow kind of skeptical reasoning. At the same time, its defensive counter-attack tends to borrow the same rationalist premises espoused by the skeptics. In approaching Scripture, for example, both follow a narrowly conceived idea of how language can or cannot be used to speak of things that permit a "knowing" not communicable in a list of facts or logical propositions. When tempted by the possibility of absolute certainty, a caution is in order, whoever is making the claim. Christians and others are at risk of being disoriented both by reductive, rationalist skepticism and the fundamentalist certainty that mirrors it.

Hurray for solar power—and for air conditioning! Society—particularly consumer society—has benefited enormously from the advancements of science: instant communication, television, film, air travel, sophisticated medications to treat once deadly diseases from tuberculosis to diabetes to HIV, and artificial intelligence, to mention only a few. We are indebted to those who first pioneered and then developed the scientific method, one of the fruits of the Enlightenment. Of course, we are less likely to be grateful for the hydrogen bomb, Agent Orange, recorded music in elevators, and, in some cases, for some of the same things for which we are also thankful. The results of scientific theorizing and experimentation may deliver to us new products that turn out to serve purposes either delightful or destructive. Once it has been created, sooner or later everything technology permits us to fashion is likely to be used. MRI machines, thankfully. But others we come to regret, whether nuclear-armed missiles, drones (sometimes) or Kalashnikovs.

The steps of the scientific method follow this pattern, more or less:

- Ask a question
- Do background research
- Construct a hypothesis
- Test the hypothesis experimentally
- Analyze your data and draw a conclusion
- Communicate what you have found

Describing your findings should enable others to test your hypothesis themselves and affirm what you have found, reject them, or call for further refinements. The process may not unfold quite so neatly as it looks on paper. It seems, on examination, to be flawless, building one certainty upon another. And yet, the method requires paying attention to a good many uncertainties, and the process draws upon both imagination and intuition.

For those of us who are not scientists, it is easy to get the impression that something like the scientific method is the only way it is possible to come to "know" anything. In fact, our whole culture has grown to share that narrow presumption. No doubt it is correct that we are not likely to know much about the physical universe, including our own brains and bodies as well as galaxies and neutrons, without making use of scientific principles and procedures. Of course, it is also possible to believe that one "knows" things that turn out not to be true. This happens even in science, when a broadly accepted theory reaches a point where the accumulating evidence of anomalies raises uneasy questions about an accepted theory. The questions may lead to the construction of brand new paradigms that address the broad spectrum of relevant phenomena more adequately. Often enough, those paradigms seem to spring into a scientist's mind intuitively, only later to be teased out and verified in a series of reasoned steps.[1]

1. Kuhn, *Structure of Scientific Revolutions.*

"Knowing" Before We Know Anything

Well and good. However, when we are thinking of matters of faith, it may be wise to remind ourselves that, although our many generations of pre-scientific forebears got lots of things wrong (the earth is flat), they were not always wrong. It is possible to "know" some things quite apart from the scientific method. For example, even before one develops the capacity to understand language or to utter a word, a child may already know a lot about belonging, love, and security. Or, in too many cases, they may already know way too much about indifference, neglect, or pain.

The very first social interaction of a newborn human being is likely to be to take nourishment. In the process, the infant engages the world for the first time outside the womb. Before there are words, there is hunger, and a repeated need to connect with whoever is likely to be responsive. If her need has not already been anticipated, the newborn soon learns to send distress messages. Even though she has no words to explain to a parent or caregiver what it is she needs, when she is hungry she announces it clearly enough with her cry, and usually nourishment appears. The baby soon learns a rudimentary acquaintance with the fact that there are others in her universe, and that it is possible to communicate one's needs to them. The answer to her hungry pleas comes from a person. The feeding routine becomes more than simple nourishment. It becomes an engagement between the one who needs food and the one who provides it. The baby, nursing or bottle-fed, locks eyes with mother, father, or other familiar caretaker. This encounter is not only about food for survival or satisfaction, but, at the same time, a basic introduction to what love, trust, and connection feel like.

Human beings "know" some things from a detached distance, when we are personally disengaged, trying to maintain arms-length objectivity as well as we can. Such detachment, or disengagement, serves us well enough when we are trying to measure the age of fossils or discover how the human genetic code works or when we are researching the number of falsehoods told by an officeholder so as to give some weight to our op-ed piece in the *New York Times*. But there are other things we "know" better when we are neither detached nor disengaged. Among them are those things we "know" even before we have language to process our experience. The child positioned at the family table will begin to discover what it means to belong without needing to see a seating chart or hear the relationships explained. At the table, we learn something about kinship or friendship—or about emotional distance—that has a lot to do with the unfolding of our basic human identity, our sense of the nature of the world and our place in it.

Babies offer only one example. Every one of us experiences more input from our environment than we are capable of recognizing and paying attention to. Lots of incoming data cannot be processed by the conscious, evaluating mind at the moment of input. There is simply too much of it. To "receive" it all at once would overload our circuits. Our conscious minds just have to filter lots of it out, paying attention only to those small bits we can absorb at the moment. But that does not mean that all the data we filter out does not affect us at some level. We "know" more than we are processing consciously, and more than we can put into words.

Detachment/Attachment

French author Antoine De Saint-Exupéry wrote a book called, in English, *The Little Prince*. It is the imaginative story of a boy who lives on a tiny planet where there is but one precious flower, for which he feels a responsibility. In subsequent travels to other small planets, he experiences a succession of personal encounters. In the course of his journeys, he meets a fox. The fox demands of the little prince, "S'il te plaît . . . apprivoise-moi . . . !" "Please . . . " The fox is seeking a deeper connection with the little prince, whom he has just met. But the prince is in a hurry. He has new friends to be discovered and things to be learned before he returns home. But the fox pleads, "On ne connaît que les choses que l'on apprivoise . . ."[2] I am quoting the French just as it is, because that verb, "apprivoise" doesn't translate easily in this context. But in the course of reading the story, one begins to intuit what it means. The fox has explained to the prince that "One only knows the things that one can "apprivoise"—only "knows" those things or persons with which or with whom one has developed a relationship. A friendship, or some other connection more than casual develops between them, even when the relationship has been necessarily brief. When the fox and the little prince finally have to say farewell to one another, they both feel a sense of loss. They had established an emotional connection that they value. The fox sums it up: "It is very simple: one only sees well with the heart. The essential is invisible to the eyes."[3]

2. Saint-Exupéry, *Le Petit Prince*, 67.
3. St. Exupéry, 71. (author's translation)

The apostle Paul, writing to the Corinthians, told them that he was praying for them "so that, with the eyes of your heart enlightened, you may know what is the hope to which he has called you . . ." (2 Cor 1:18). Of course, the heart has no "eyes," but even a hard core literalist might understand that Paul is saying that there are some things that are accessible to us only from a position of attachment. To see some things, we may be better positioned if we are more or less detached, of course. This may be true for the judge interpreting the law; the psychoanalyst treating a patient; the biologist, anthropologist, or historian studying the human race to learn how and why we have become what we are. But, for other things, we are better positioned to see when we are emotionally and personally attached.

If it is good to be able to discern the unhappiness, disappointment, or grief of another, it will require laying aside a defensive indifference so as to permit ourselves to feel something of what the other feels. Remarkably, even a small child is usually sensitive to the emotional temperature of a room, whether it be warm and stable; or chilly, tense, and prone to outbursts. As we mature, we can easily develop imperviousness, if it suits us, deciding not to register emotional states of people around us, for the sake of our own peace of mind. To notice and to care may certainly put us at risk of having to share a measure of another's distress. And yet, empathy is not only desirable when we ourselves are in need of it, but to be able to experience it in the case of another opens us to dimensions of relationship that provide satisfactions otherwise unavailable. It simply feels good to reach out to another in a caring way: listening, a touch of the hand, simple availability. All these utilize parts of the self meant to be used. Detachment, in such cases, serves well neither the neighbor nor ourselves. Empathy is a kind of "seeing" with the heart—a "knowing" that is subverted when reduced to a technique.

To discover a capacity for empathy is not something that we ordinarily learn either by having the need for it explained to us, nor by being argued into it. It comes naturally, rising up out of someplace in us that is accessed not by intellectual probing, but by trusting "the eyes of the heart." And yet, one could reasonably object that empathy will get us into trouble. It may disturb our emotional equilibrium, it may require of us an investment of time and resources for which we have not made an allowance. Since empathy may not always clearly serve our own personal interests, it may be the case that the "eyes of the heart" have led us to where we don't want to be, and that detachment, disengagement, might better serve what we perceive to be our own wellbeing. Thus, we consent to disable or at least minimize a natural capacity for relationship, usually to our loss.

Two Ways of Seeing

Like empathy, faith in God is not ordinarily learned simply by having it explained to us, or by being argued into it. Like a capacity for empathy, faith may also rise up in us apart from any calculated effort of our own. Also similarly, the phenomenon of faith may be critiqued, noting that it may get us into trouble, and that, whatever evolutionary use it may have served, it might be prudent now to turn away from it. Detached, rational, systematic analysis—i.e., the scientific method—can be liberating because it might be less emotionally risky, right? Less likely to get us entangled where it might cost us something?

There are many arguments that intend to make a case for the "existence" of God. None of them is airtight, just as none of the many arguments *against* the "existence" of God is airtight. Every reasoned argument has to begin from some premise, a beginning point presumed to be foundational; i.e., not subject to empirical verification. Both the believer and the unbeliever embrace one of these premises without either demonstrable proof or an unassailable argument: God is, or there is no God. Both the scientific method and philosophical methods are based on a presumption that a detached impartiality is necessary to adjudicate theoretical questions. Some, no doubt, on either side, have been swayed by arguments, even changed their minds, discarding one foundational premise and trading it for the other. However, I don't know anybody whose faith is the result of a well-made argument. To be intellectually persuaded that God "exists" is not the same as having faith. Arguments may help to clear the way for those who are already inclined toward faith or against it. But faith does not depend on reasoned arguments. It is more akin to ways of "knowing" already accessible to an infant.

Emotional "knowing" probably evolved in living creatures, including human beings, far earlier than the ability to reason analytically. In that sense, it might be called "primitive," but only in the sense that it is ancient—part of our original equipment. It is no less real, no less useful than the ability to form a reasoned judgment and, in fact, it may often enough prove to be more accurate. When rationalizations overcome the data provided by our emotional compass, it is not always because the emotional compass is deficient or has misled us. The rationalizing itself might be suspect, perhaps a process of useful self-deception. Attachment—a personal emotional investment—is less useful when it comes to adjudicating testable facts, but can be quite useful in assessing and forming relationships. When we presume to resolve the question of God, for which the answer really matters, we are not in the realm of testable facts, but of relationship.

Detachment and attachment are two quite different ways of engaging with that which is real, but made manifest in different ways. To understand how to make and find uses for a laser requires detachment. To understand one's most basic relationships, one's place in a larger world, as well as one's relationship to God, requires something more like attachment than detachment. It is possible to get anything wrong, whether in those matters requiring detachment or those best discerned from an attached perspective. In neither case are we guaranteed the kind of certainty that never requires any second thoughts.

Both detached "seeing" and "seeing with the eyes of the heart" require a measure of trust. One way trusts the impersonal method of scientific investigation; and another way trusts those levels of experience that cannot be measured and quantified. (And it is important to be able to know which is which!) To be "known," invisible dimensions of reality require the engagement of the whole self: emotion as well as reason; intuition, too, particularly an informed, knowledgeable intuition. "Knowing" involves learning to tune in to the wavelengths of those unconscious signals given and received in our human and natural environments. Faith is confident that there are dimensions of reality that, while invisible, are yet equally important as those that are visible. Sometimes, even more important.

A Sacramental Universe

One of the strengths of both Roman Catholicism and Orthodoxy is that those communities are experienced in cultivating a "sacramental" sense of the universe. I am not referring to the church's sacraments as such, although they would be included, but to a way of experiencing material reality as a means by which the glory of God may be communicated to us. One might argue that this sacramental sensibility is also a weakness. It can lead to trouble, as it clearly had done on the eve of the Reformation. To value the material world as a vessel in which the spiritual may overflow into our awareness can lead to a distorted over-evaluation of a material object. In other words, it can lead to superstition. Examples might be the veneration of the knucklebone of a saint, or imagining that one might steal a wafer consecrated for eucharistic use in order to weave a magic spell.

The sixteenth-century Reformers were shocked by such superstition, and understood that it needed to be countered. They countered it with words. Words from the Bible, words of preachers and teachers, words in printed catechisms, and books that could be easily mass-produced once Gutenberg's printing press replaced the need to copy manuscripts by hand one at a time. This way of confronting superstition by explanation and explication served a purpose, but, magnified by the Age of Reason that would follow not long after, it morphed into an over-correction. The material world came to be seen as "merely" material—understood as *not* spiritual— a neutral object to be manipulated or exploited, but not a vessel for communication of the holy. Water is only water, oil only oil, bread only bread, wine only a fermented drink. Stripped of the expectation that it might serve as a means by which the glory of God might be made manifest, the material world became seen as a neutral zone, mostly separated from the transcendent. Except perhaps for a lovely sunrise, a mountain or ocean view, the material world was more easily perceived as a sphere of indifference to the question of God's presence or absence, particularly so among Protestants.

This was true even though the Reformer John Calvin had imagined the universe itself to be the "magnificent theater" of God's glory.[4] To discern the world as a theater of God's glory, or to perceive the material world to be a sacramental vessel capable of communicating the holy, represent more or less the same vision, a similar insight. However, the need to push back against superstition, and the wordiness necessary to support the essentially cognitive effort to do it, had the effect of capitulating to the Enlightenment-influenced banishment of the sacred from any manifestation in ordinary physical things.

Roman Catholicism today has not abandoned its sacramental sense of the creation, but it is certainly not anti-science, and it does not normally encourage superstitious ways of perceiving or manipulating material things. (Not always the case in popular piety.) In some quarters, Protestants have also begun to reconsider the remedies offered by the Reformation when they appear to have over-corrected. The material world, as well as specific substances within it, may be perceived, under the right circumstances, as a non-verbal witness to God.

4. Calvin, *Institutes*, 341.

It would be an over-statement to claim that the very fact of the existence of the universe proves a Creator. Such an argument would not be able to withstand a serious debate. The Protestant Reformers themselves understood that so-called "natural theology" has limitations. The universe itself, with its order and its discernible patterns, may testify to a Creator, but one may nevertheless appreciate, enjoy, and learn from the natural world without seeing the hand of a Creator. To describe human beings, John Calvin used the image of an elderly man with failing sight. This man sees the world and senses its Creator in and behind it, but only senses, dimly. He does not see clearly. The picture is blurry, open to misperception until he puts on the spectacles that bring into focus what has always been before his eyes.

God's Sacramental Beckoning

The spectacles, in Calvin's telling, would serve as an analogy for the Bible, with its various testimonies by which we perceive God's disposition, character, and larger purpose. And yet, to shift the analogy, what the Bible does is not only to focus the mind's eye, but to provide a place of meeting between God and human beings. That might just as well be described as a *sacramental* encounter. In any language, the same words may be used both for the sake of science and in service of faith, but they will be used differently. The words of the Bible are employed in a variety of ways, sometimes just as they are used for every day practical matters and sometimes mingled with images and metaphors one next to another, each serving to correct, balance, and nuance the others. And sometimes, biblical language makes use of poetic devices. They don't explain so much as they evoke in and from us something that has always been there but never surfaced to the point where we could either feel it unambiguously or examine it. The Bible is not a user's manual as much as a sacramental phenomenon. In other words, one in which God may use an artifact with human fingerprints all over it as a vessel with which to meet, touch, and engage with us. Ordinary things— even words strung together by human beings—may be made to serve God's purpose and desire to connect with us in heart, mind, and soul.

Scientists tell us that the universe is suffused with something described as the electromagnetic spectrum. One piece of that spectrum is composed of light that is visible to the human eye. Other pieces—x-rays, gamma rays, microwaves, radio waves, infrared, etc.—are not ordinarily visible to us. This ever-present radiant action, filling every bit of the universe since its originating moment, surrounds us even though we are not usually conscious of it or thinking about it. By analogy, a sacramental view of the natural world would permit us also to imagine that material reality may become a vessel for God's self-revealing, even though God, by definition, is not a part of the created universe. Here and there, now and then, in and through the testimony of the material world that constitutes our earthly environment, we may catch a glimpse of God who desires to be made known. Scripture, for example, makes use of human language as though it were a lens to help us see more clearly what we might otherwise easily miss.

That the material world itself testifies to the glory of God implies that, in some sense, God becomes knowable to all human beings as naturally as becoming aware of one's own breathing or heartbeat. As the infant encounters all sorts of discoveries about love and relationship just by taking nourishment, God is also as near to us as the atoms that compose our bodies. But of course one can unlearn love, or come to doubt it. One can disable the capacity for relationship, and dismiss its possibility cynically. And, one may ignore God's sacramental beckoning, doubt it, and dismiss it. The precognitive sense of the divine is not meant to overpower us, and it is fuzzy, ambiguous, unfocused. Nevertheless, there are those who, sensing the divine, may feel a desire to awaken to it; to see it more clearly. God has not created us to hunger and thirst for something that does not exist. God has made us to desire deeply what God stands ready to give: God's own self.

The gospel's testimony is that in Jesus Christ, God has come to meet us, to satisfy the most urgent desire of the heart, and to assure us that the fullness of "knowing" our Creator is yet to come. But how can we hear anything that directs our attention beyond the conventional and ordinary? In our era, we are constantly bombarded with impressions that drown out subtler signals. Silence has become rare. We are tethered to hearing devices and screens almost 24/7. With our conscious minds constantly preoccupied and distracted, our sensitivity to the presence of the divine underlying the material world has become muted. Numbed, but not entirely disabled.

Trying on a Pair of Glasses

Faith is always a response to some stimulus. It is not merely closing one's eyes and taking a leap into the dark. One of those basic stimuli, though subtle, is the sense that beneath it all there is some lively presence. Somewhere, somehow, we sense that there is something—Someone?—who knows us better than we know ourselves. Who knows our own personal history, including even all that we have forgotten. Who sees us in all the complexity of our multiple relationships with people, communities, and objects, including our rootedness in the material world. This intuitive sense of being known may not be registered consciously, may not be something we have actively thought about or put into words. Nevertheless, it is there, part of our original psychic equipment. Human beings are just set up that way.

Even in those cases in which we recognize that we are taking for granted some unseen but lively presence that transcends every day reality, it does not mean that we have faith. Pollsters ask people whether they "believe in God." A remarkable number are willing to say that they do. But it is easy to declare that one believes in the proposition that there is a higher power. That may mean that one trusts God, but it need not. To believe *that* something like God exists is not the same as having faith *in* God. Faith is a big step further than mere intellectual consent to an idea.

An anonymous deity whose reality may be sensed intuitively and casually acknowledged lacks definition. How could anyone trust a deity whose character is unknown? There is more than one way to conceptualize a deity. It may be theorized that "God" is the watchmaker god, who wound the universe up, set it in motion, but appears to have lost interest. One can at least conceive of a deity for whom the universe and every form of life in it serve as playthings, with no more serious value at all. Or, commonplace enough, the deity's main interest may be in laying down rules and punishing those who don't follow them. No human capacity exists that is able to investigate deity directly and report back with even a basic character reference. Unless God makes the first move, we are left with only empty speculation.

Of course, Judaism, Christianity, and Islam all claim that God has, in fact, made the first move. Each believes that God has reached out to human beings in acts of self-revelation. Islam is persuaded that God has self-revealed in the specific language of a book, the Qu'ran, given directly by God in Arabic, and authoritative only in that language. Jewish and Christian sources use biblical narratives, parables, devotional language, moral and ethical commands, water, bread and wine among other means, to unwrap what is given in God's acts of self-revelation. The Christian gospel develops themes already present in the Old Testament, but presses further. The Christian gospel is that the person of Jesus Christ—not just what he taught or the Bible itself—is the embodiment of God's self-revelation.

God is known in Jesus' humble birth, his act of identifying with sinners when he was baptized by John; known in Jesus' ministry to the broken, the scoff-laws, and the aliens; known in Jesus' death alongside those who are cursed; known in his resurrection that serves as a promise that God and God's will shall ultimately be made manifest throughout the whole, transformed creation.

To move from an intellectual nod to the likelihood that there is a God and then to the point of actually professing faith is a move that requires help. The help comes from a community that shares its story and gives shape to the otherwise shapeless sense of a deity otherwise anonymous and unknowable. The community tells its story, using whatever verbal and non-verbal modes the story requires and the community finds useful. The person who comes within the reach of their story may try it on, as the old man with failing sight tries on a pair of glasses. The story "fits" when it brings into some sort of orderly focus the breadth of one's experience. The story "fits" when it touches them in those places where only the divine touch will do. It "fits" when one is given words with which to speak coherently of One whose reality and presence had been sensed, but incoherently. To determine the fit rests on some of the same sorts of intuitive receptiveness we see in the child learning about love, security, and belonging as she takes nourishment offered by a caring parent. But the halting language necessary to put that into words has to be learned, and we are taught it with the help of the narrative supplied by God's self-revelation in Christ, to which the Bible bears witness and the church testifies.

Feeling the Beat

Sometimes faith begins to spring up in response to an experience of beauty. For example, a sunrise, or light playing on a garden, children laughing as they run in chasing games, the sight of one's newborn child or grandchild, the serenity of someone who has accumulated a lot of years. Some report something like a mystical experience, a sense of the harmony of the whole, a dawning confidence that we are neither alone nor entirely on our own.

In Mary Ann Taylor-Hall's novel, a young woman named Carrie is powerfully drawn to a young musician named Cap. Carrie says,

> When Cap and I sang in harmony, something happened. Our two voices—well, they sounded good together. They slid together trustfully, they were of one mind. The harmony was all instinct,

his voice just found the right place for itself against mine, through every last little edgy turn. Harmony's all there is or needs to be, when it's right. It was like dancing.[5]

"All instinct," was the harmony. Carrie and Cap's harmony flowed in part out of their attraction to each other. Love is always searching for its own music. It seems also to be the case that those who find themselves met and claimed by Jesus Christ discover something like their own music. It's like dancing. One feels the beat. It fits.

In sharp contrast, sometimes faith springs up in response to a crisis. We come close enough to death to see clearly and directly our own mortality, without any ability to avoid it, control it, or even accept it. Or, faith may spring up when our lives have been derailed. Our own weakness, neither chosen, detected, nor effectively combated, led to alcoholism, drug addictions, and the kind of behaviors necessary to support them. Family in disarray, personal ambitions crushed, instability the norm. From the bottom of a pit we hear a word that turns the heart. We see light for the first time in a long time, or maybe ever. We come to "see," to "know" what had before seemed to be either nonsense or entirely irrelevant.

Of course, for some, faith is simply their normal state of being. It always has been. They have been surrounded by it and affirmed it themselves from the beginning of their lives, and, though they may have questioned it and even argued with it, they have never completely lost it. Their stories are likely to be less dramatic than the stories of those with a stunning mystical experience or a turnaround so complete and so shocking that not even those who wished the best for them ever expected such a thing.

The parable of the man with two sons demonstrates the possible contrasts (Luke 15:11–32). The younger son feels cramped in his father's household. He boldly asks for his inheritance, as though he cannot wait for his father to die, and heads off to the big city. He not only breaks free of the values of his family, but turns his back on Torah and even basic decency. When things go badly, he comes to his senses and returns home, where, amazingly, his father welcomes him lavishly. The older son has never left home, never given his parents a moment's trouble. He has followed all the guidelines, respected the tradition in which he had been formed. When his father welcomed back the prodigal brother so generously, the older brother became bitter, but the father assured him that he was equally loved. In terms that might be transferable to more recent examples: we see the

5. Taylor-Hall, *Molly Snow*. 107–8.

notorious sinner, who now makes a "decision for Christ," contrasted with the hard-working brother who has always been in church on Sunday, trustworthy, having kept the faith all along, although perhaps a little bit smugly. Equally loved.

Hope

For the person in whom faith has been kindled for the first time, or in whom it has been rekindled after having faded or been forgotten, the experience of faith may feel like bliss. In that first state of bliss, it feels as though one has discovered something transformative—a mystery that unlocks hopeful expectation—and one wonders how so many can possibly be unaware of it. Of course, bliss under any circumstances is a temporary condition! But the substance of it persists over time, having morphed into something more enduring than a strong emotion. The substance of the experience of faith has to do with the kind of hope that undergirds one's whole life, coexisting, when it must, even with states of depression and anxiety. Hope, in this case, is not wishful thinking or a permanent high, but it is a kind of "knowing," a knowing of God that rests on confidence that God is sure to have the last word, and that such a word can only be a good one.

At bottom, the gospel understands faith to be a response to a question we may not have even known we had. A question about where we shall entrust our very selves, in life or in death. The prophet Isaiah, speaking for the holy God, called out, "Turn to me and be saved, all the ends of the earth! For I am God, and there is no other" (Isa 45:22). This is also the testimony of the gospel, to which the church adds its own, pointing to Jesus Christ, "the reflection of God's glory and the exact imprint of God's very being . . ." (Heb 1:3).

Of course, every person of faith has a story to tell, each at least a bit different from all the others. It is possible to describe situations and processes that, seen in retrospect, had the effect of leading to faith. But at bottom, faith is unexplainable. It is a mystery (not the same as a problem to be solved). We tell our stories and describe processes as a kind of effort to explain to ourselves where faith came from. In ways sometimes perceptible and often imperceptible, God seems to have prepared us for something we may or may not have been looking for, and may or may not welcome, and for which we may or may not be able to find our own words.

God can be trusted. For those who welcome it, faith is normally experienced as a gift. It is not in our power to manufacture it. Faith is a kind of "knowing" that is occasioned by a "seeing" somehow enabled when the "eyes of the heart" are opened, whether we had intended that or not.

3

Faith

I ask no dream, no prophet ecstasies,
no sudden rending of the veil of clay,
no angel visitant, no opening skies;
but take the dimness of my soul away.

— GEORGE CROLY

Faith not a Claim to Certitude

IN A CULTURE IN which faith has been understood either as a claim to ab-solute certainty on the one hand, or silly superstition on the other, thought-ful Christianity rejects both. When faith is a challenge, and even regular churchgoers are not sure whether they have it, how to get it, or whether what they have is enough, it becomes necessary for us to think seriously about what faith is not and what it is. Faith is a matter of basic concern for all Christians, not just for those who presume they are the only ones to have it.

Letting it slip that one has faith in God is more risky than it used to be. Whether intended or inadvertent, it will not always be welcomed or taken for granted as normal. Still, now and then, someone will say to someone suspected of being a believer, "I wish I had your faith." Often this simply means, "It must be comforting to believe that, but . . ." (often unspoken) ". . . I can't and I don't." Although such a statement may be only a polite brush-off, it can also be a sincere lament. What is faith? What would a person have to do to get it?

The hypothetical person envious of faith may mistakenly understand it as though those who claim it must be in possession of some hidden and mysterious certainty that is not available to everyone. And presumably such certitude rests on some dynamic experience that has led to uncluttered confidence. Perhaps it was a personal spiritual experience, a voice or a vision, a transcendent encounter of a mystical sort that is beyond any objective questioning. Or, on the other hand, it may rest on a powerfully persuasive intellectual argument that may or may not be communicable to someone of an uncertain frame of mind. Lacking similar certitude, how can faith be possible for the one who has had no unambiguous authenticating experience?

One may be understandably suspicious when hearing someone claim that their faith rests on an unquestioning and unquestionable certitude. Even when one feels confident, confidence does not rule out doubt. In all sorts of matters, one can be confident even while acknowledging the possibility that one may be wrong. For example, a non-scientist may feel relatively confident that one day it will be possible to replace lost parts of the human body—say, an arm or hand or leg—with a prosthesis that functions almost exactly like the original. Based on recent advances, it seems reasonable to expect such a development sooner or later. Even non-scientists might reasonably be confident about it, even though they have absolutely none of the expertise that might suggest how such a thing might be accomplished. Even though there is always room for doubt, confidence may be a reasonable stance even when one is not positioned to claim absolute certainty.

Faith and doubt are not mutually exclusive. In fact, doubt can be a useful servant of faith, causing one to dig deeper, to search for elusive connections, to engage objections that help to clarify what is at stake. Without the experience of doubt, it is easy enough to settle for a faith that is untested and carelessly framed, less than adequate to meet the challenges of real life and careful thought.

Faith Challenged

For most people, faith is likely to be challenged most profoundly by life experience rather than by intellectual contests. To live is to run the risk of being hurt. There are losses, and relationships ended; there are failures large and small, disappointments that leave one suspecting that the game of life is rigged and terribly unfair. Such experiences are not likely to be much affected by theoretical arguments in God's defense. Some people lose faith; others feel justified in never having had it; while others wrestle with God and accuse God and discover that even though the relationship with God has been rocky, it is still a relationship.

One pastor, having completed a pastorate and begun another, was surprised to receive a letter from Ms. A, a woman he remembered well. She had become a member of the congregation he had once served, and wrote to bring him up to date and report on a recent achievement. She reminded him that he had met a chilly reception when he had come to her apartment to meet her after she had wandered into worship one Sunday. She was a widow, with a science background, who had created a science-based business and made a success of it. She had had one grandson, already grown, who worked in the business with her. He was the apple of her eye, and they were close. In fact, both had a taste for science fiction and were in the process of writing a sci-fi novel together when, suddenly and unexplainably, he died. When the pastor of the church she had visited had paid a call, she remembered having poured out her story, and made it quite clear that she was angry at God. In her letter, a few years later, she reminded him that he had told her that he had come to tell her it was okay to be angry with God.

Her letter reported that she had finished writing the sci-fi novel that she and her grandson had begun together. It took a turn, however, that was entirely her own. People from the planet Earth had landed in a world where they found living beings who did not look like them but were otherwise similar in sensibilities. Wide-ranging exchanges brought one of the travelers from the planet Earth to mention God. When questioned about how he would describe this God, he responded by showing them, on his phone, a photo of Michelangelo's Pietà, a figure of the crucified body of Christ in the arms of his mother. This is what God "looks like." In other words, God's person has been made manifest in the godforsaken Christ. The God who is in Christ will always be found in the cross-shaped places, of which there is no shortage, ever.

Ms. A had had the novel published and sent the pastor a copy. She had wanted him to know that her anger at God had been transformed without having been necessarily repudiated. Anger was part of a larger emotional picture, and no longer required her to turn her back on the God whom she had met when she found herself lost in an unanticipated cross-shaped place.

One might reason that a person who feels injured by the circumstances of her life is a fool not to follow her anger to its logical conclusion: atheism—whether based on true conviction or as an attempt to punish God for perceived dereliction of duty. Nevertheless, counter-intuitively, Ms. A's experience is not new or unique. It has been replicated many times over the generations. To be angry with God and to charge that God is doing a poor job of running the universe does not always lead to repudiating God. In fact, in many cases the very intensity of emotion leads to or at least permits a deeper embrace.

> We are afflicted in every way, but not crushed; perplexed, but not driven to despair; persecuted, but not forsaken; struck down, but not destroyed; always carrying in the body the death of Jesus, so that the life of Jesus may also be made visible in our bodies. (2 Cor 4:7–10)

One can either be entirely cynical about what seems like inconsistency, or one can permit oneself to imagine that faith, like any sort of deep relationship, is capable of coexisting with a certain amount of mystery. All relationships are dynamic, not entirely predictable even when we have a good sense of the other's character. Every undertaking and every relationship is susceptible to unknowns. And surely it is safe to presume that God's ways are not our ways. At bottom, the point would seem to be that faith in God is a living thing, not merely a single cognitive transaction—either "I believe" or "I don't believe," decided in a moment and that's all there is to it.

Other than Intellectual Assent

Our conventional understanding of the uses of language have been powerfully influenced by rationalism of the sort that has become dominant in Western cultures since the Enlightenment, the so-called Age of Reason, dramatically reshaped ways of thinking. Reason has come to equal a kind of semi-mathematical reduction of language to a logical argument. When we hear "faith," it is easy to hear it as though it had to do with an intellectual act, a rational exercise of the mind. The same is even truer of the word "believe." When we ask what some person or movement or institution believes, we expect in response a list of propositions that appeal to our reason. A proposition may be affirmed with or without deep personal engagement. For example, "I *believe that* having a religious faith might be good for some people."

Believing *that* some position or argument is true is a different use of the word than when we say that we believe *in* some person or institution or movement. Intellectual assent—believing *that*—may be hot or cold, passionate or indifferent. Believing *in* is always more holistic, engaging both heart and mind. I believe *in* my spouse, my attorney, the person who does my taxes, my teacher, my neighbor, my government, my child, my church, my God.

The word "faith" can be used similarly as, for example, having faith *in* some person, group, or cause. For the church, both—faith *in* or belief *in*—when they apply to God, imply a relationship of trust. They are personal, not impersonal. They engage the whole person emotionally as well as intellectually: heart, mind, and will.

To believe *that* there is a God may be nothing more than intellectual assent to a likely proposition. When that is the case, it may not be too difficult to be talked into it or out of it. Or, it may be a deeper and more personal engagement—belief *in*—in which case one is less likely to have reached that point by having been talked into it and less susceptible to being talked out of it.

The experience of faith in God is not unreasonable, but it is other than simply the product of a series of logical steps. Falling in love is not unreasonable, but neither is it the result of a reasoning process. For example, a parent may question why their daughter loves this person she's brought home rather than someone they may presume to be a better match. She has finished medical school, an internship, and a residency, and fallen in love with a young man who is a registered nurse. Her parents find no special reason to dislike the young man or question his character, but they had imagined that their daughter would marry another doctor, or a lawyer in line for partnership in a large firm, or at least someone with a high profile job and good prospects for financial advancement. They are disappointed. They try to reason with her. Why this guy?

But, even if their daughter manages to come up with a list of reasons that make a case for the potential partner's lovability—among them some mix of looks, athleticism, sense of humor, sexiness, intelligence, culinary skills, devotion to her—even taking all of these characteristics together doesn't explain it. The supporting reasons supplied to the questioning parents came to the daughter's mind *after* she had fallen in love. The list of reasons was an afterthought, not a cause. Love makes sense to the lover, but it's a sense that can't really be transferred to anyone else, not even to those who may recognize and appreciate from an emotional distance the personal strong points of the beloved that could be included in the "pro" column of a pro and con list.

A Movement of the Heart

Similarly, a list of reasons that support the reality of God will not, by themselves, evoke faith; i.e., love for God and a desire for a relationship. It does not matter which column of reasons on the pro and con list turns out to be longer. Like love, faith is a spontaneous, intuitive, and unorganized response to an "other" to whom our attention has been drawn. When a person falls in love, reasonable arguments in support of one's choice of this particular person are not likely to serve a purpose except to shore up a movement of the heart already made. Likewise, faith comes first, while reasoning to justify it, if found necessary, follows. In quite the same way, a state of disbelief is likely to precede the accumulation of arguments gathered to support one's spontaneous skepticism.

This sequence—commitment of some sort followed by the development of supporting arguments—is not unique either to falling in love or to the experience of faith. At almost every level of life, the sequence is the same: experience first, reasoned support later. Loyalties to people, movements, parties, economic theories, tribes, scientific paradigms, alma maters, ideologies, theologies, and anti-theologies nearly always follow the same sequence: an initial personal, intuitive, and precognitive commitment supported by reasons after the fact. Of course, facts and arguments can undermine commitments and challenge reasoning, so people sometimes do change their minds and withdraw or redirect their loyalties. Clearly enough, reasoning matters, but it's only a piece of the story.

Since, with every kind of personal engagement, some sort of trustful connection comes first, rather than reasoned arguments, where does faith come from? How might one get it? If "get" means finding a technique to acquire it, there is none. The church has always understood faith to be a gift, not an accomplishment. And yet, to desire it enough to be sincerely interested in how one might experience it is a likely indicator that some small seed of it has already been planted.

How might such seeds be planted? It is wiser to avoid laying down categorical rules, since faith may very well manifest itself quite unpredictably. Nevertheless, experience indicates that most often faith results from some human encounter. The encounter may begin in infancy or childhood, with a faithful parent, grandparent, or nurturing community. Or it may emerge at any age as a way of making sense of an observation of someone or some community whose faith has been exhibited in action, demeanor, or even in words. Even a lone individual with no prior knowledge of Christianity, happening upon a Bible and becoming absorbed in it, encounters communities of people—Israel and the church—in and through what she reads. The Bible emerged out of and for those particular communities of faith, and has been preserved, pondered, and handed on by those communities—Israel and the church. In any case, faith is always the result of some kind of personal encounter, whether direct or indirect. It is never "blind," but always a response to some sort of stimulus. It is not just a gamble, recklessly throwing oneself into the void.

A staff member in a downtown church had the responsibility of planning and leading the annual Confirmation class. Anyone who has had a similar experience knows that working with thirteen year olds can be a joy, but almost as often proves stressful. As they prepare young people to be confirmed, adult leaders can't help wondering what is in their minds. The one who has been brought to church regularly by a conscientious parent committed to the faith might be expected to embrace the experience and reflect the parents' faithfulness, but it doesn't seem to be happening in this case. Instead, the adult leader of the class encounters someone who brings a grudging and foot-dragging presence of the kind that signals coercion.

In another case, however, the staff member reports that the experience was quite the opposite. A member of the Confirmation class had been brought to church by her mother once in a while, motivated both by a half-hearted sense of obligation and a feeling that her daughter ought to be exposed to some sort of religious education. The girl's father was a member of a non-Christian faith, though he was not observant. The girl felt pulled in by her experience in the class, took seriously what she was encountering, and, now a senior in high school, recently dropped by to tell the church staff member that she was interested in considering the ministry. From being a detached observer just going along with the program, she had come to see herself as included in the narrative centered in Jesus and discerned in the nature of the relationships she discovered in church as well as in the story that animated it.

A Gift of the Spirit

God sometimes finds those who, so far as they themselves know, aren't looking for God. In the case of Christianity and Judaism, at least, faith is most often kindled by narratives and the community that springs from those narratives, including encounters with communal ritual. It is not, of course, inevitable that people exposed to the narrative and/or to the worshiping community will all respond in the same way. Some, exposed to another person's narrative of experience, or to the biblical narratives handed on by the church, or to the church's worship will find themselves indifferent or decisively rejecting it all. Such rejection once again illustrates the intuitive sense that faith cannot be commanded, controlled, or engineered by the use of some technique with a guaranteed result. It can best be understood as a gift, even though that affirmation itself makes us wonder how and why some receive it and some don't.

The Gospel of Matthew records an incident in which Jesus was querying his circle of disciples, wanting to know what people were saying about him. They reported some popular theories about his identity, which prompted him to ask them where they stood. "But who do you say that I am?" Simon Peter answered,

> "You are the Messiah, the Son of the living God." And Jesus answered him, "Blessed are you, Simon son of Jonah! For flesh and blood has not revealed this to you, but my Father in heaven." (Matt 15:16–17)

Not a very satisfying observation for one who would like to know the details, but it tends to square with experience. As Jesus said on another occasion in reference to the Holy Spirit and its fruits, presumably including faith, "The wind blows where it chooses, and you hear the sound of it, but you do not know where it comes from or where it goes" (John 3:8).

If faith does not usually rest on some sort of mystical experience that evokes certainty, or on an unassailable argument sufficient to overcome any objections, then on what does it rest? An easy answer, in this age of explaining everything either by evolution or by psychology, is that faith results from psychological influences, originating from sources either external or internal to the individual. That is a reasonable supposition. Either faith results from the influence of people and communities and authoritative voices in our environment, or from one's own personal issues and struggles, or from both. The interaction of our DNA, life story, and various environmental influences tilt us toward faith, or against it. That is likely the case.

Yet, in the language of Bible and church, we may still say, using a kind of theological and linguistic shorthand, that faith is given by the Holy Spirit. One of these ways of speaking does not rule out the other. In fact, the Spirit may very well work in, by, and through human processes that can be studied and described without reference to faith. It is not as though faith can only claim legitimacy should it have been given like a sort of supernatural transfusion or spiritual electric shock quite apart from the biology and psychology of human beings and their societies. We are mortal, formed from the dust of the earth (Gen 3:19), or, in other language, formed from atoms, or even from the most basic components of atoms. God created us using the materials of the physical world. God reaches out to us, becomes known to us, making use of the physical substances and dynamic processes by which human life has evolved.

Faith emerges, sometimes where we are likely to look for it and sometimes where it is entirely unexpected. Faith, it seems, can also be lost, and sometimes found again. Faith occurs among those whose thinking is simple, lacking all complexity; and it occurs among the intellectually gifted. Its intensity varies over time as it encounters challenges and finds ways to respond to them.

Everybody Has "Faith"

Trying to explain the phenomenon of faith is a project that has its limits. The experience of loving someone and trying to explain that love to a third party can only go so far. To experience, on the one hand, and to explain experience, on the other hand, involves moving between two different emotional and linguistic universes. For example, a student in a Social Studies class may encounter a unit on religions of the world. A Jewish student may agree that the section on Judaism in the textbook is technically accurate. The Muslim or the Christian may say the same about the material on Islam or Christianity. And yet, when a person who experiences the faith of a community from inside it encounters the arms-length description of a writer whose goal is to be accurate while of necessity personally neutral, the description seems somehow to be off. Something is missing, and what is missing is not so much information as experience. Written in prose, the affirmations of a faith seem crazy, or pedestrian, or irrelevant. A different sort of language is required to communicate the essence of faith—one that is in tune with the melody of it, the poetics, that can only be intuited, not explained in a textbook's required mode of objectivity. It is necessary to experience faith for it to make sense personally rather than just intellectually.

Of course, when the Bible speaks most profoundly, it does so in a poetic voice. Yet, even the work of the artist whose medium is words can seem ridiculous when verbally evoked images are mistaken for journalistic language. The phenomenon of faith can be explained in a way that makes sense, but not in such a way as guaranteed to evoke faith. Faith emerges as a response to stimuli that can be simple or complex, and those stimuli vary from person to person. Faith is an answering response to something (Someone?) made present to us, faintly or strongly. The pastor calls out to the congregation, "Lift up your hearts!" The congregation responds, "We lift them to the Lord!" And that is what faith is. It is an uncalculated lifting of the heart. A vibration in response to the divine heartbeat. The heart rises toward the God who reaches out to us in Christ by the Holy Spirit. Then follows the reasoning, the doubt, the questioning of one's own self, and a process of working out this heart and head relationship over a lifetime.

Faith may seem a curious affair to one who has no experience of it. And yet, faith is not rare, nor is it confined to people who belong to churches or other communities of faith. When one loses faith in God, a vacuum remains that demands to be filled. Lost faith is likely to be replaced by something else that promises to fill the void. One finds oneself in search of something that at least appears to be similar to what's been lost, something calling for a high level of devotion. For example, these days an easy substitute might be a nearly fanatical sense of certainty in politics as has ever been on display in either fundamentalism or atheism.

Faith is a positioning and a process that describes resting one's trust, one's confidence, in some person, object, idea, or community. Easily enough, the objects of our faith (our "gods," if you will) are likely to be the panaceas, the ideologies, the persons, symbols, and institutions we love, but from which we are prone to expect more than can possibly be delivered. We are likely to be disappointed, because they fall short of their idealized versions, or let us down at the crucial moment. There are deceptive "gods" in whom we center our lives, only to become disillusioned. Some of them offer what not infrequently turns out to be a kind of pyramid scheme, promising high gain at low cost. These "gods" may be the close at hand substitutes to whom we pledge our loyalty in hope that they will realize often extravagant expectations.

The daily newspaper carries obituaries, more and more often for people who apparently belong to no religious community, but who nevertheless appear to have placed their faith in something: tennis, motorcycles, pets with cute names, an *alma mater*, professional distinction, a lengthy list of good deeds and honors, the flag, whatever. Broadly described, everybody is likely to have some kind of faith, and not just people who gather for worship in a church, mosque, synagogue or temple. Whatever the object of one's faith—of one's trust, confidence, devotion—no faith commitment is more easily explainable than another. Why such a commitment to saving prairie dogs or butterflies? Why did identifying with the state university's sports teams prove so important to someone's sense of identity? The explanations for such, if there are any, are not such as to be likely to evoke the same devotion in someone else. Faith of every kind is both explainable and not explainable. To the extent that it is explainable, the explanation nevertheless does not make the experience of faith easily communicable.

The Divine Signature in Capital Letters

The message entrusted to the church is framed in human language, earthbound speech formed to describe earthbound things. And yet, the biblical narratives use this mortal language ingeniously, this way and that, both straightforwardly and indirectly, to communicate God's call and God's promises as manifested specifically in Jesus. It has proved effective in countless generations and cultural settings. Who can explain the amazing pull of the gospel?

One may try to explain it by making a list, just like the smitten daughter can probably come up with a list of traits trying to justify her already established love for the person her parents might not have chosen. Such a list might include the testimony that wherever Jesus goes, one sees signs of a world being repaired. He names and calls out those who misuse their authority, whether secular or religious. He brings the shunned, the "unclean," in from the cold. In Galilee or Judea, when he encountered someone without sight or hearing, unable to navigate their environment easily, he opened up their world. When someone's body didn't work, or bore some contagion, he clothed them with health and strength. When he met a person tormented by unstable thoughts and perceptions that made them frightening to themselves and others, he brought clarity and calm. Death was denied the last word, grief overcome, tears noticed and tended to.

Wherever Jesus is present, God is writing the divine signature in capital letters, promising that what we see happening in Christ is a down payment on the way things shall be. In word and action, Jesus is the embodiment, the representation of what the world looks like whenever God's new creation is made manifest. God's kingdom, God's reign, God's dominion appears a little at a time, here and there, now and then; but one day, it will be manifest everywhere, not possible to miss it. In Jesus, we see into the very heart of God as clearly as it's possible for mortals to see. We catch a glimpse of God's disposition towards us, otherwise unknowable. Jesus is that sure point in which there is no guile, no self-serving, no deception or self-deception, no falsehood, no distortion, no unkindness—truly our north star. "You will do well to be attentive to this as to a lamp shining in a dark place, until the day dawns and the morning star rises in your hearts" (2 Pet 1:19).

That glimpse is enough for some to support a lifting of the heart such as focuses the mind, filters out distractions, and encourages the taking of that first step that leads to lifelong discipleship. As Jesus said to the twelve, "You did not choose me, but I chose you" (John 15:16).

It is perhaps at this point, when one finds one's face turning toward the God whose character and disposition have been disclosed in Christ, that we discover the need for a mentor, a coach to orient us to the Christian life. Remember how it works: experience first, reasoning to follow. In those moments when one detects a stirring of faith, the questions begin to emerge. How do I explain this? To myself, or anyone else who asks? Obvious objections to faith make themselves felt. Who is God? How do we dare think we know enough to say anything at all about God? What's the point of it anyway? How do I nurture the new faith that I have? What should I do next? The church is equipped to offer a mentoring role, and ought to be challenged to learn, in this new era, how to take that role seriously.

Sometimes we need to borrow faith. Ours is weak, challenged, in peril, or even apparently absent. In such instances, we are in search of support, and that support is most likely to come from others whose faith is, at the moment, strong enough, unthreatened, and not immediately at risk. They may be a family member, friend, a congregation, or even the anonymous faithful, aware or unaware of our personal struggle. Their faith holds us up when we don't have the strength to do it ourselves. If, strengthened by their faith, we continue to assemble with the worshiping church, continue to maintain our customary spiritual disciplines however difficult it may be, the faith we borrow usually resurges, whether sooner or later. Then, in reciprocation, it may become our turn to lend faith to those who find it wanting in themselves. This is what it means to share the life of a community of faith, and there is no shame in it. We borrow, and then we lend, each in turn as circumstances require.

4

The Faith of the Church

To be sure, even believing that the church has in fact made it this far,
that there is now an actual church to worry about, means trusting in
the Spirit's past action to preserve the church in spite of itself,
in large part by the instrumentalities of canon and creed.[1]

— ROBERT W. JENSON

Communal Faith

IF ONE WERE TO substitute the word "trust" for the word "faith," it would
almost work. Yet, the word "faith," like some other English words, can be
used in more than one way. It is possible to speak of the Islamic faith, the
Jewish faith, or the Christian faith. When used in that way, the word "faith"
refers to the whole ecology of communally held beliefs, doctrines, and
practices.

Christian faith is always held in community. It is not just the sum total of private opinions or practices. As mentor and coach to those new in
the faith, whether baptized children or adults who have just come to faith,
the church is responsible to show and tell. Showing and telling includes
exposing those new to the community to the faith of the church—in other
words, to the teaching and practice that flow from the basic narratives that

1. Jenson, *Canon and Creed*, 118.

58

form the spine of both Old and New Testaments; teaching that has served as the basic material or content that Christians have pondered, discussed, debated, and handed on from generation to generation; and practices that mark our common life.

When no mentoring process exists, whether formal or informal, those who somehow find themselves in the church without mentoring are forced to try to figure it all out on their own. Lacking anyone to help them learn how to understand the communal language of Scripture, doctrine, and worship, they quite naturally move to form their own ideas of what is meant by the apparently simple three-letter word "God," for example. Not to mention sin, salvation, incarnation, etc. Because we live in a culture that defers to language that sounds something like scientific or technical reasoning, they are likely to improvise idiosyncratic explanations that answer to those expectations but suffer from serious distortions. Anyone undertaking a Christian confession both needs and deserves what is sometimes called "catechesis"—i.e., a guided exploration of how the church understands, embodies, and hands on its own shared faith.

The process of the church's mentoring includes, of course, helping novices to make their own what belongs to all. To make it one's own requires wrestling with it, examining it from the viewpoint of one's own life and experience, discovering the connections and puzzling over the disconnections, and doing all that in conversation with the mentor(s) and, through them, with the whole universal church.

And what's the point of such exercises? To be new to faith is like being new to music or to mathematics. You may be intrigued by hearing music, and may yearn to play jazz or Bach, but before you can compose you have to learn the scales and train yourself to coordinate the mental and physical actions necessary to make such music. With mathematics, it's necessary to start with simple arithmetic and advance from there. Working out complex mathematical problems comes later. Faith is utterly simple, in a sense, but because it has to relate to multiple experiences and a world in which reality is complex, if we are going to take it seriously enough to inform our life in the world, we have to explore it in depth and at length. Our mentor, the church, like our music or mathematics instructor, can work with us so that we need not encounter the issues or challenges as though no one has ever encountered them before, and model the ways we use and understand the language of faith. Our mentor can also alert us to very real threats to faith that have surfaced now and then in history and may still be alive today, even though we may not have recognized them, or encountered them yet.

Faith Seeking Understanding

A shorthand word for the content of the faith shared by the church is "doc-trine." Doctrine is not a rule or a law to which one is obliged to conform. It is, rather, a human attempt to bring as much focus and clarity as pos-sible when speaking of God and holy things. Doctrine is the product of the church's careful reflection on its experience, including the experience of prophets and apostles as characterized in the biblical narratives and reflected upon by other biblical writers, as well as by later generations of pastors and teachers. Doctrine is a sort of "portable narrative," a "folded-up story" to use the words of New Testament scholar N. T. Wright.[2] The nar-rative behind the doctrine is the story itself. Doctrine is the material of the teaching church, reflecting on the story.

Doctrine has usually emerged in response to some precipitating mo-ment, whether questions arising from debate or conflict, a challenge com-ing from the culture or from within the church, or questions that arise when people encounter the gospel for the first time, or from a social crisis. Some doctrine is fluid, involving questions frequently discussed but never resolved. The most basic doctrine is that which has, over time, earned a consensus among most Christians. Examples of basic doctrines would be creation, the incarnation of God in Christ, Holy Trinity, the cross and res-urrection, and God's ultimate dominion, the "kingdom" (*basileia*)[3] of God, or new creation.

Doctrine is meant to be illuminating, to add intellectual depth and dimension to our faith; to remove obstacles that stand in the way of faith; and to expose more clearly how God and our faith in God relate to the complexities of human experience and thought. Doctrine sheds light on how we might fruitfully position ourselves in and for each other and the world. Nevertheless, on first encounter, a doctrine may seem only puzzling, particularly when, as is often the case, it is meant to answer a question that has occurred to many but not yet to me. To be puzzled is useful when it arouses our curiosity (or resistance) and opens up the possibility of further conversation, exploration, and a willingness to go a little deeper.

It is often the case that the puzzle will not be solved so simply that we can without reserve either affirm a doctrine straightaway or deny it

2. Wright, *Day the Revolution Began*, 223.

3. *Basileia* is the New Testament Greek word for "kingdom." Used here in place of "kingdom," "reign," or "dominion."

outright. We find ourselves relating to it differently than to some fact or opinion about which we can easily and without much wrestling simply make up our minds. Better to come to terms with the fact that our best option is to recognize that some doctrine needs to be pondered for a lifetime. One reflects on it forever, with the various seasons and experiences of life providing a whole series of perspectives, each from a different angle. Viewed from one angle and then another, each opens up a possibility not considered earlier. Why doesn't it all come clear once and for all, sooner rather than later? Because the affirmations, illuminations, challenges, and connections cannot be seen or experienced all at once. Doctrines testify to things that are so rich and layered that they are not easily comprehended without necessary and even prolonged reflection. They illuminate various aspects of experience that we may not yet have encountered personally.

Doctrines are interpretations of the unsystematic narratives upon which both the Old and New Testaments are structured. Their purpose is to assist us as we draw from the narratives all that they continue to offer in helping us understand the world, ourselves, and the God who is at work in both. Their role in the church is to keep at the center of our focus what belongs at the center of attention: God's presence and action in Jesus Christ crucified, risen, ascended, his resurrection serving as the promise of a new creation in which all things come together under his sovereignty.

Navigational Beacons

It is neither unusual nor scandalous to struggle with one or more of these affirmations, whether we meet them first in the biblical narratives or in the form of an interpretive doctrine. The object of faith is God, and the substance of it is trust in God, not belief in a doctrine as such. Belief in a doctrine is not a sort of test—a challenge with which God is trying us. Nor is it a prerequisite that we need to produce in exchange for God's favorable disposition to us mortals. Belief in a doctrine is not a way of paying for a ticket to heaven. Doctrine is useful when it serves to lead us to a closer relationship with God and a deeper understanding of what that means and where it is pointing us. God does not turn away from us when we struggle with a doctrine or find ourselves afflicted by doubt.

Doctrine, wisely used, is a gift. It is a tool useful to the church as it mentors those in its care. Doctrine takes us by the hand and shows us things we need to look at. God does not scorn us if we don't get it. Jesus

Christ is at the heart of the basic doctrines of the ecumenical church. It is Jesus Christ with whom Christians have to do. Because, in the church's experience, doctrines direct us to him, our part is to weigh them respectfully rather than make hasty, first-impression judgments. A modest suggestion would be to summon the patience and personal discipline to live with these basic, ecumenical doctrinal affirmations in the hope and expectation that, over time, they will become more and more transparent to us, showing us clearly enough the One we need to see when we most need to.

Churches—especially those most directly linked to the sixteenth-century Reformation—are likely to make use of creeds and confessions of faith to guide teaching and mentoring in the work of interpreting the substance of the faith. Creeds and formal, written confessional documents are not infallible, nor are they, in themselves, the objects of faith or the point of it. Nevertheless, they help to keep us anchored in those basic biblical narratives that require reflection and interpretation particularly as cultures and contexts change over time. Tom Long has chosen just the right images when he writes about "the capacity of ancient creeds to serve as navigational beacons in the still-moving river of faith seeking understanding."[4]

When idolatries of every sort exercise their seductive pull on us, with either explicit or implicit scorn for the biblical God, the church may find itself tempted to substitute some sort of generic deity for the difficult one who meets us in Scripture. When we hold on to the navigational beacons represented by the creeds—particularly those creeds confessed by the larger part of the ecumenical church—they serve to keep us on track when pressed between fundamentalist absolutisms on the one hand and religious skepticism on the other. The creeds direct our attention to the biblical God whom we take to be above all other claimants to the name.

Faith—the experience of a trusting relationship with God—is experienced within a community that cherishes and hands on a tradition, one form of which is doctrine; i.e., simply a way of saying "teaching." The "faith of the church" has specific content different from other faiths, whether they be secular, religious, or simply "spiritual." That content furnishes and supplies the church's ministry of teaching and mentoring. Its ultimate goal is to mark out a path for discipleship, supporting a resolve to walk hand in hand with Jesus Christ. The search for faith will begin, perhaps, by turning our attention to the most basic thing of all: the communal faith that draws us

4. Long, "Binary Christianity of Marcus Borg."

to and unites us with the God who is, whether we recognize it or not, the object of our longing.

With Angels and Archangels

To "know" the Christian faith in an unscientific but nevertheless real way of "knowing," it is necessary to give oneself to the practice of worship in Word and Sacrament. For those who really want to sense the pulse of a living faith—which is the only way to "know" it—worship is the place to look for it. Worship is where we turn our faces toward the One who is our true north. In worship, we respond to God's call.

When God ("I AM") appeared to Moses and self-identified by means of a bush that was burning but not consumed (Exod 3:1–6), the initiative was God's, not that of Moses. Isaiah also offers another example among many of God making the first move.

> But you, Israel, my servant,
>
>> Jacob, *whom I have chosen,*
>>
>> the offspring of Abraham, my friend;
>
> you whom *I took from the ends of the earth,*
>
>> and *called* from its farthest corners,
>
> saying to you, "You are my servant,
>
>> *I have chosen you* and not cast you off . . .
>
> (Isa 41:8–9, italics added)

Similarly, Jesus' disciples did not choose him. He chose them. And so it goes through the generations of those who are called to faith, and called to worship. It is God who calls. We answer. And God is in both movements.

The Orthodox churches believe that their liturgies make it possible, in a sense, to enter the gates of heaven while still on earth. In other words, worship offers a meeting place where human beings are lifted for a time into the presence of God. This is an elevated way of speaking about what is, by observation, quite mundane. In worship we engage in prayers, song, listening, movement, silence, and sacramental acts. The meeting place may be quite ordinary; the people ordinary; the words ordinary; and the water, oil, bread, and wine ordinary. It is in the shelter of this ordinary that God has condescended to meet us, just as God condescended to meet Moses in the burning bush and meet disciples in the ordinary man from the ordinary town of Nazareth.

When one assembles with the church for worship on the Lord's Day, it is as though one has moved from a narrower world into a larger one. The narrower world of the other six days is not very narrow, actually. It includes all the encounters of daily life, including the up-close encounters and the at-a-distance ones. It includes all the politics, all the popular culture, all the traffic, the landmarks, the off and on ramps, as well as whatever is online, anywhere, everywhere. But on Sunday, with the church, the boundaries quite unexplainably expand to include Adam and Eve (so to speak), Moses, the parents of John the Baptist, the twelve disciples, Lazarus and his sisters, the Marys, Joseph of Arimathea, and, of course "choirs of angels, prophets, apostles, and martyrs, and all the faithful of every time and place."[5] And it includes all of those for whom we offer—or ought to offer—our intercessions. Gathered in worship, the world of here and now also includes there and then and what is yet to come. We discover the boundaries of the temporal pushed back to offer a glimpse of the broader spiritual universe and to experience it for a moment as what it is: our ultimate home and our home now, bigger and roomier than we can imagine.

At the very same time, gathered with the usual folks and maybe some new ones, one often asks oneself whether this can really—really?—be the body of Christ. And here is where it is necessary to call upon the power of holy imagination. Not making something up, but seeing beneath the surface. Yes, this is the body of Christ, even though it includes me, and even though we don't all look like the kind of recruits one might have thought to have been chosen for the team. "You did not choose me but I chose you" (Jesus speaking, in John 15:16).

Classroom or Meeting Place?

If any of these things are true, then it would seem that there is a lot at stake in this weekly assembly. The Roman Catholics and the Orthodox agree that worship is at the center of the Christian life, referring in their cases specifically to the Mass or the Divine Liturgy. Protestants are not always quite so clear about that. A mother who had fallen into the habit of worshiping only occasionally announced to the family that they would be going to church next Sunday because it was Easter. Her nine-year-old son complained

5. Presbyterian Church (USA), *Book of Common Worship*, 70.

that he had no need to go to church, because he already knew what Easter meant—it was about the resurrection. In other words, he had already learned the lesson linked to the day, as though worship were a classroom softened by a few aesthetic touches for those who appreciate them. Tomorrow will include a trumpet or two, lilies, and lots of choir. But to conceive of Christian worship as a classroom is to misconceive it. No doubt the nine year old also knows what his birthday means. Since he already knows that birthdays are a way of counting the years, will it prove sufficiently satisfying to him just to hold that in mind? Would he be okay just to skip the exercises organized around the date? Not bother with the assembling of his family and friends, the singing, the candles, the cake, and the presents? If so, what dimensions of experience would he miss?

Traditionally some have roughly equated Sunday, the Lord's Day, with the Sabbath. In the past, the Puritan Sabbath often implied support for blue laws, regulating what sorts of public activities should be permitted on Sunday as well as expecting church members to observe the day quietly, with worship both public and private, at its center. Those days have passed, and, with more and more encroachments of activities formerly reserved for weekdays now scheduled on Sunday, it is hard to say what the day means for us. It is also hard to say how earnestly we ought to contend for members to guard times for Sunday worship and study. It has become commonplace to define regular attendance at worship as once or maybe twice a month. Weekly participation seems no longer to serve as the norm, and, as always, minimum expectations sooner or later become the maximum.

If the assembly for communal worship is, for practical purposes, no longer considered the center of the Christian life, then what is? And if it should be so considered, how ought we to handle Sunday conflicts with sports practices, scheduled games, social events, etc., whether for children or adults?

The second of those questions requires ongoing discussion. Practical issues will require practical remedies. However, I do not believe that it is safe to lay aside the claim that the assembly for worship is central to the Christian life. Worship is not about communicating information, a lesson for students to master. It is in the active assembly that the body of Christ is made manifest in a context of witness to the resurrection—thus Sunday rather than Saturday. And it is here that God provides the essential nourishment that sustains every other facet of the Christian life. Here is where God meets not just assorted individuals, but a community chosen to serve corporately as God's "royal priesthood" (Exod 19:6 and 1 Pet 2:5, 9). And it is that assembly that meets God with words and gestures of the sort exchanged between partners joined in love.

Two Values: Flexibility and Consistency

The language of worship is loaded language. It is loaded with presumptions about God—who God is, how God has acted to be made known, and what we may say with confidence of God's character and disposition towards us and the whole world. To speak of the "language" of worship refers, of course, to specific words and how they are arranged, but also to non-verbal kinds of "language"—movement, gesture, tone, the arrangement of the people in relation to each other and to the furnishings necessary for the central acts of worship, and often also color, light, and symbolic messages communicated by or within the space itself.

A visitor to a service of worship may be quite puzzled, depending on how much experience the visitor brings to it. One engaged enough to be tuned in will certainly form some sort of impression of the deity to whom the community is offering its thanks and praise as well as its petitions and intercessions. In other words, the basic foundations of faith are on display, represented in what is said and done in the worshiping assembly. Which is to say that the specific affirmations of the church's faith—its core teaching, its theology in fact—is embodied in its worship quite as much as it is embodied in its creeds, confessions, and academic theology. The form is different, of course, but the substance is the same.

Because this is the case, it is puzzling when churches treat what is done in the worshiping assembly with less care and interest than they are likely to treat their official theology. And yet it is likely that what is actually done in the service itself makes at least as deep an impression on the worshipers as the sermon. If a church is interested in receiving what God is ready to give in this intentionally intimate encounter, as well as building on what it has received, it needs to pay a lot of attention to its primary assembly for worship.

Liturgical flexibility, characteristic of much of Protestantism, can be a strength. A weakness of Roman Catholic and Orthodox practice is that both are less flexible. And yet, one could take the words "strength" and "weakness" in the two sentences and trade each for the other, and both would still be true. Liturgical flexibility, like all the other kinds of flexibility, gives room for appropriate local adaptations. At the same time, it opens a door for all the limitations and misconceptions possible in local cultures, tastes, and experience, as well as deficiencies in knowledge. The greater the flexibility, the greater the risk that cultural pressures will manage to have the last word.

Less flexibility, on the other hand, is a weakness in that the liturgy is not as likely to be closely attuned to local cultures. For the same reason, less room for flexibility can be a strength. The Mass, for example, is recognizably the same everywhere. Not only does it have the same shape and order, but even the words (as far as vernacular differences allow) are the same. However, the music may be different. Some of the movements and rhythms may be different. The Mass can look and feel different in Africa than in Indonesia, in an African-American parish than in one that is primarily Irish- or Italian- or Mexican-American. By keeping flexibility within bounds, the resulting upside is a commitment to basic consistency. Whatever the cultural setting, such consistency provides a persistent continuity that is less vulnerable to being overcome by local influences incompatible with the substance of the faith itself. Such consistency is a value that is available alongside considerable flexibility when we are willing to learn from the service books of several mainstream Protestant denominations.

The Divine Heartbeat

Sometimes it is not the words themselves that matter, but the way they are used. For example, the Apostles' Creed developed as a baptismal confession. The Nicene Creed was formulated to address major issues that emerged in early centuries and needed resolution, and it later came into use in worship as a kind of accompaniment to the Eucharist. Lutheran and Reformed churches used either one in worship, but were particularly drawn to the Apostles' Creed.

The value of the creeds, of course, is that they touch base with the foundational biblical narrative and related theological affirmations of the faith. Even earlier than the twenty-first century, however, many mainline congregations began feeling discomfort with the creeds. Discomfort at first in the wake of the reductive rationalism that accompanied the Enlightenment; and now also, when many congregations have had little or no experience with either teaching or preaching that exposits the benchmark affirmations of the creeds. Cultural dissonance contributes to that lack of familiarity as religious skepticism becomes more public, and congregations may not seem to be ready or willing to be patient with the challenging affirmations of the creeds. When the creeds are used in worship, it may seem as though the congregation is mumbling the answers they have found in the back of the book. One may sense a lack of energy, an absence of conviction. But the experience can be quite different when the Creed is sung. When joined to music, the same words are experienced differently. Some intuitive sense is more likely to kick in, so that we know without being told that we are not reciting a set of opinions we have either agreed upon by personal research or have had imposed upon us.

During the liturgy for baptism, a Presbyterian congregation already acquainted with more than one metrical version, sang a text of the Apostles' Creed by David Gambrell set to the tune of Genevan 42.[6] The tune is lively, rhythmic, and forward moving, but in this case made even livelier accompanied by two hand held drums beating the rhythm. The congregation rises to the occasion, and the palpable energy of the singing clearly communicates the Creed's doxological character. In other words, it was not the dutiful recital of a lesson but an act of praise and celebration. The congregation experienced the Creed, and, one may imagine, experienced some sort of holistic encounter with the God to whom it bears witness. A receptive encounter, perhaps, with the divine heartbeat. This, too, is a kind of "knowing."

Intersection of Past, Present, and Future

Presuming that the assembly for worship on the Lord's Day is meant to represent and embody the substance of the faith, which is to say God's identity, character, and disposition toward the world, the prayers require attention. For example, are there prayers of intercession? If there are not, the long-term effect will be, by omission, a misrepresentation of God's character and the breadth of God's interest and compassion. If there are, who is included? One may hear prayers for known members of the congregation, either by broad category (sick, grieving, rejoicing) or by name (often first name only). But are there prayers for categories of people not members of the congregation, but who are in the news today and this week? Victims of natural disasters, human-caused atrocities, economic crises, either in our own country or far away? Those struggling with homelessness and those

6. Presbyterian Church (USA), *Glory to God*, #481.

who work with them, the hungry and those who feed them, those afflicted by extreme heat or cold? Does the congregation pray for those in positions of governmental authority, and if so, by name—including the President, Governor, Mayor, whether popular or not?

What God do the faithful "know," recognize, and honor in the prayers of the liturgy? For a congregation to be able to extend its prayers beyond its own boundaries and beyond familiar parochial and tribal boundaries is essential not only for its own sake, but also because the choice of who will be included in our prayers is not arbitrary, but entirely rooted in what we have been given to know of God's basic character. How does the God revealed in Christ and served in the church become manifest in the praying congregation? Will God's graciousness, God's love, and God's judgment (calling us and injustices of the whole world to account) be recognizable in our prayers? How do our prayers form us over time, and what do they say about our God even to casual observers, let alone the seriously curious?

When the liturgy of the church is faithful to the God who calls it to worship, it opens up to a broader vista than an ordinary gathering does. It offers a glimpse of a "communion of saints" that includes people who are present in the assembly, faithful who live far away, and many who have gone before us, transcending the boundaries of time and space. It becomes, by the power of the Holy Spirit, "catholic." To be "catholic" is to recognize a kinship in Christ that transcends "tribal" boundaries, whether economic, social, racial, ethnic, gender, partisan, sectarian, national, geographic, or even temporal. And, when it is faithful to the God who calls us, the liturgy of the church leads us to find ourselves in a moment in which past, present, and future meet and intersect.

It is easy enough to recognize the past in our worship. We read from the Bible, an ancient book written originally in Hebrew and Greek, composed at particular times and places by and for people of different cultures and frames of reference from our own. We speak of Jesus Christ, whose itinerant ministry in Galilee and Judea occurred twenty-one centuries ago.

And, in the assembly for worship it is easy enough to detect that the church understands itself to be obliged to be attentive to the present. It will be announced that the youth group will meet to plan their summer mission trip. Volunteers are needed to participate when it is our turn to provide hospitality, meals, and shelter for a group of persons struggling with homelessness. We pray for them and for those who have been afflicted in this week's list of natural disasters or mass shootings. We look expectantly for Christ who meets us in the sacrament.

If this particular mainline congregation pretty much makes up its own liturgies week by week, either unaware of denominational resources such as a service book, or aware but not interested, the overlap of past and present may not include the ultimate future. And yet, if the congregation prays the Lord's Prayer, they will be familiar with the words, "your kingdom come," even if they have no idea what that is supposed to mean. Should they make use of the Apostles' Creed, they will have heard the words, "from there he shall come to judge the living and the dead." The Nicene Creed is a nice combination of both: "He will come again in glory to judge the living and the dead, and his kingdom will have no end." However briefly, the liturgy that includes Lord's Prayer or creed does, at such a moment, point to God's future.

Remembering the Future

For a good many Christians, past and present are more comprehensible within the framework of the faith than is the future. Should they be inclined to think about the future in ways specifically formed by faith, it may be that they will identify the future with "heaven." "In the future, I will die and I will go to heaven." Or, if they are more interested in the social justice implications of their faith, they may identify the dreamed-for future as the ideal one that may result from our determined efforts to make the world a better place. "Together, we are building the kingdom of God."

Whether it be "going to heaven" or "building the kingdom," one may see in either vision of the future something of Jesus Christ and his gospel. And yet, neither quite begins to do justice to the biblical vision of the future. However, if this hypothetical mainline congregation is one that either makes use of a denominational service book, or even uses it only by fits and starts, they may have heard words like this in celebrations of the Lord's Supper/Holy Communion/Eucharist.

> Eternal God, we unite in this covenant of faith, recalling Christ's suffering and death, rejoicing in Christ's resurrection, and awaiting Christ's return in victory.[7]

Or,

7. United Church of Christ, *Book of Worship*, 48.

70

By your Spirit make us one with Christ, one with each other, and
one in ministry to all the world, until Christ comes in final victory
and we feast at his heavenly banquet.[8]

These prayers for God's *basileia* are a traditional part of the eucharistic
prayer, or Great Thanksgiving. They are a petition for the fulfillment and
manifestation of God's ultimate rule. The two quoted come from service
books of the United Church of Christ and the United Methodist Church,
but can also be found in similar liturgical sources published by the Presbyterian Church (U.S.A.), the Evangelical Lutheran Church, the Episcopal
Church, the Reformed Church in America, and no doubt others.

When the liturgy of the church includes both Word and Eucharist, it
embodies, at least theoretically, the essentially forward movement of the
Christian gospel. That forward movement was evident from earliest times,
exemplified in the assembly for worship not on the Sabbath, but Sunday,
the day of Christ's resurrection. Sunday is technically the first day of the
week, but because it was also the day of the resurrection, early Christians
identified it also as the "eighth day" in anticipation of the fulfillment of
God's new creation beyond ordinary counting of the days. The accent is on
God's future, as promised in the resurrection of the Lord.

Sacrament of the *Basileia*

Of course, for the earliest Christians, nothing was more basic to their
assembly on the Lord's Day than a shared meal. (Acts 2:42; 20:7; 1 Cor
11:17–33) The meal included time for spoken reflections on Jesus, his
ministry, his death and resurrection and his promise of a new creation in
which he would be actively present. No doubt the assembly also reflected
on texts and narratives from the Jewish Scriptures, our Old Testament, that
contributed to shaping the people's perspective on what the phenomenon
of Jesus in his ministry, death and resurrection might mean.[9] The larger,
all-embracing context for such first day/eighth day reflections, and the exhortations, encouragement, and consolations that flowed from them, was
the meal.

8. United Methodist Church, *United Methodist Book of Worship*, 38.

9. "Old" Testament need not mean obsolete; rather, it can just as easily acknowledge
seniority. In any case, "Hebrew Scriptures," often used in printed orders of worship, is not
quite accurate, since the books are arranged quite differently in the Jewish Tanakh than
in the Christian Old Testament.

Since then, Catholics, Orthodox, and Protestants have, in distinctive ways, often broken apart or distorted the relationship between that part of the meal in which the Word is read and interpreted, on the one hand, and that part that is the thanksgiving/eating and drinking on the other. Preaching became marginalized among the Roman Catholics and the Orthodox. The meal has been marginalized for most of Protestant history. Post-Vatican II, Catholics and Protestants have experienced parallel attempts to recover the lost unity of these two interrelated and essential poles of Christian worship on the Lord's Day, moving toward convergence from opposite directions.

Orthodox theologian Alexander Schmemann has made very explicit what one might otherwise miss: the liturgy shaped by those first-generation Christian assemblies was one thing in two integrated movements, Word and meal forming an indissoluble whole. All of it together from beginning to end is the Eucharist—not just the Great Prayer and the eating and drinking. The Eucharist/Holy Communion/Lord's Supper is what Schmemann calls "the Sacrament of the kingdom."[10] In other words, it serves as a kind of down payment on the *basileia*, the promised heavenly banquet. "Then people will come from east and west, from north and south, and will eat in the kingdom of God" (Luke 13:29). When our Lord's Day Eucharist is complete, it directs us to God's ultimate future. "Blessed are those who are invited to the marriage supper of the Lamb" (Rev 19:9).

We remember the past: "Do this in remembrance of me" (Luke 22:19b). We discern the past as present to us: "This is my body, which is given for you" (Luke 22:19a). And we turn our eyes to the future: "I tell you, I will never again drink of this fruit of the vine until that day when I drink it new with you in my Father's kingdom" (Luke 26:29).

The Renewal of All Things

Basileia might best be characterized using a phrase Jesus used, as "the renewal of all things" (Matt 19:28). Whenever Christians lose this sense of God's purpose as a universal, cosmic renewal—a "new heaven and earth"— it is easy to find ourselves sliding into an individualistic framework where all that matters is me and my salvation. Or, to imagine that God's purpose is something we can effect if we are only determined enough, "building" the *basileia* piece by piece, as though we should actually be able to construct

10. Schmemann, *Eucharist.*

one finished piece that will actually stay nailed down while we move on to the next project, then the next, until it is all finished at last.

It is clear enough in the New Testament that God is calling human beings to do something—to play a role in imagining and making manifest the *basileia* here and there, now and then—even though it will always be God who is the definitive actor. But human beings being what we are, the result of our construction skills might just as easily look more like the Tower of Babel. We are what we are: confused, at odds with one another even when intentions are pure. Yet God calls us and makes use of us, even though in ways we cannot precisely describe or understand. And so we pray, in confidence that God is trustworthy, for Christ to come again in final victory and do what we cannot do all by ourselves: realize the *basileia*.

The *basileia* is the ultimate image of the Christian hope. Not just my salvation or yours, one at a time, each of us on a solitary journey. Not just a project we shall surely master if only . . . Not identifying any political party or cause or movement or any ecclesiastical maneuvering in the direction of a theocracy as though one of these could be the leading edge of the *basileia*. That way leads to arrogance, authoritarianism and catastrophe.

So we hope, we anticipate, we see beyond the horizon to God's work, a healed and mended creation, where there shall no longer be either prey or predator.

> The cow and the bear shall graze, their young shall lie down together; and the lion shall eat straw like the ox. The nursing child shall play over the hole of the asp, and the weaned child shall put its hands on the adder's den. They will not hurt or destroy on all my holy mountain; for the earth will be full of the knowledge of the Lord as the waters cover the sea. (Isa 11:7)

Images from both testaments picturing unlikely reconciliations and unexpected celebratory banquets for those not ordinarily inclined to mix are images that are capable of helping us to imagine more clearly what God has in mind for us to do even now. To do now, insofar as possible, in order to bring into being some state of affairs—here and there, now and then—that may somehow at least roughly resemble the *basileia* to come. Imagining the world in anticipation of its transformation, using the vivid biblical images as lenses, enables us to see our own world, our own time, more clearly. How do cutthroat partisan politics look from the vantage point of the *basileia*? How useful does it prove to be to divide "winners" from "losers"? Whose interests are served by constant plotting to subvert the interests of other nations, other races and tribes, other religious communities? How will a plundered world, polluted, subject to weather extremes, inhospitable to its many species of plants and animals honor the hope of a new creation? The biblical images of God's *basileia* offer to mind and heart images of what life might be like when everything is in balance. The God in whom we labor to trust is a God whose intention is to rebalance the world so that it will look something like the picture of Jesus among the poor, the sick, the wounded, the outcast and the downcast. Or resemble the biblical images of the river of life that sustains fruit-giving trees that produce leaves for the healing of the nations (Rev 22:2). Or even a picture of the dead, rejoicing, having been visited and liberated by the crucified Christ who "descended to the dead" (1 Pet 3:18–20).

To point to the *basileia* and anticipate its inauguration in the same Christ who visited us in Galilee and Judea may seem ridiculous. It is beyond the possibility of mortals to imagine a world reconciled and in balance except as we use the fragile tools of human language to speak indirectly and inadequately of what cannot be spoken of directly. To speak at all of the "second coming," and the resulting *basileia*, requires the help of an artist. Biblical artists use words to paint verbal pictures of something never seen and not easily imagined except as we see it modeled in Jesus Christ. The biblical images point us in the right direction despite their lack of technical detail in the manner of scientific or historical description. As we *remember forward* we sense that we are in touch with a hope that is rightly placed in the God to whom the ultimate future belongs. A hymn text set to the popular tune "I'll Fly Away" invites us to imagine that future, the *basileia*.

> When the Lord redeems the very least . . .
> . . . restores the sick and weak,
> . . . revives the world from death,
> . . . returns in victory,
> . . . we will rejoice.[11]

The Cosmic Dimensions of the Christian Hope

Apart from the vantage point provided by the promised *basileia*, it is easy both to distort the Christian hope and for such distortions to shape (or actually misshape) our worship and, with it, narrow the scope of our perception

11. © *1991 GIA Publications, Inc.*

of God's purpose and mission in Christ. Often the scope is narrowed so that it is no larger than me or you, and our own personal destinies. Or, that God's purpose is to gather some people whose purpose is to be role models for others, with all the risks of developing the kinds of smug superiority (or desperate sense of failure) that implies. The gospel itself may be perceived to be no more than guidelines for living a moral and ethical life, with no attention to the bigger picture, a cosmic redemption. Whenever the broad parameters of God's salvation are narrowed, however they may be, it is both a misperception of the grand scope of the gospel promises, and certainly a loss of that broad and broadening perspective.

The very flexibility so often characteristic of much Protestant worship, however useful, can easily become a liability when local option is taken to an extreme. When either Eucharist/Holy Communion/Lord's Supper or even preaching is occasional, or when the classic themes embodied in the eucharistic prayer are unknown or otherwise left behind, the cosmic focus of the Christian hope is easily lost. When no ecumenical creed is professed, or professed only now and then, it is likely that only the Lord's Prayer will remain to testify, doxologically, to our hope in the *basileia*. And it is not unthinkable that even that prayer may be used only occasionally by some Protestants. In any case, if presence in worship only once—maybe twice—a month is the standard for "regular" attendance, then exposure to prayers and creed will be significantly reduced.

In some churches, repetition is considered to be evidence of a lack of sincerity. Novelty supposedly demonstrates reliance on the Spirit who presumably has no use for widely shared historic liturgical patterns. Where this disposition holds sway, it will not seem to require attention to theological detail as worship is planned and executed. Ritual studies, however, find that repetition matters.

> A ritual that contains repetition within its structure, such as the repetition of words or actions, facilitates the internalization of the ritual's content in many ways . . . Reiterating the same gestures and the same formulas in identical circumstances and following a fairly regular periodic rhythm, it implants the values of the group into the body of each member.[12]

For liturgy to be effective, it has to be repeated to the point of familiarity. Even so, the relatively brief articulations of the Christian hope, of remembering forward, may not make much impression on worshipers

12. O'Donnell, *Remembering the Future*, 162–3.

without directly reflecting on eschatological[13] themes as texts and seasons permit. Until that happens, the references to the *basileia* will likely serve mainly as placeholders until the time comes that someone will carefully draw attention to them. In that case, they are not lost or abandoned, but waiting to be noticed. This holds true as well for Catholics and Orthodox as well as to those Protestants who have, or are recovering, a liturgical tradition.

Sacramentally Abled

The present moment is an ambiguous one. On the one hand, some Christian groups have narrowed these affirmations of redemption on a cosmic scale to something like a scenario of simple reward and punishment. Some get all the reward, others get all the punishment. For them, Christ's coming in glory acquires the character of a threat that marks a dreadful impending division. "In case of rapture, this car will be driverless," the bumper sticker boldly testifies. This narrowing is another example of stumbling over the nuanced language of Scripture, reading it as though it were a direct and objective description of things that in fact are beyond human capacity to describe directly.

The ambiguity here is that, in some quarters of ecumenical Christianity, the eschatological vision—remembering forward in anticipation of the reign of Christ, the *basileia*—is being recovered. And, such recovery is beginning to make itself felt in our hymnals, in our sacramental prayers, in text-based preaching, and in teaching. And yet, of the two tendencies—unnecessarily literalizing, on the one hand, and recovering the cosmic breadth of Christ's redemption on the other—the literalizing version has, over the long run, gotten more attention, much of it not in the least positive. The risk of being identified with the literalizers can intimidate those who perceive the truth and beauty of the biblical vision, even causing them to back away from it.

Our culture has developed in such a way that spiritual truth that might, in other circumstances, be intuitively accessible, just as artistic creations channel truths that are intuitively accessible, is no longer. The culture of the past four hundred years or so has brought many good things, but it has also nearly incapacitated our ability to make use of intuitive skills as we

13. "Eschatological" refers to the ultimate future in which God renews and recreates all things.

process the images and affirmations of the gospel. Even a statement of faith must meet expectations equivalent to a scientific demonstration. Anything of serious importance must be presented as though from an objective distance in order to be taken seriously. If a theological affirmation requires borrowing poetic, suggestive, and intuitive language rather than being laid out only in universally accepted propositions, it does not pass the test. To pass the test presumably requires of us something like neutrality, indifference, and detachment.

A husband and wife had a grown son in his twenties. The young man was intellectually disabled and lived at home with his parents. Their custom was to be present for worship at their church on Sunday mornings. One Sunday, for some reason, the parents decided the family needed to stay home. The father told their son that they wouldn't be going to church that day. The young man was quiet for a long time, pondering. And then he broke his silence to ask, "Won't Jesus miss us?"

One may find his question touching, but naïve. However, one might also consider that his question—"Won't Jesus miss us?"—tells us how the young man experienced worship. He perceived it as a kind of meeting with Jesus. It was not about processing information, mastering a lesson, learning the rules, hearing it all explained. It was about *presence*—what one might call the sacramental presence of the risen Lord in the gathered community of the faithful. In other words, his disability in processing information analytically, critically, was not so highly developed as to obscure his ability to experience the divine presence. In the case of many if not most "modern" people, our ability to be "sacramentally-abled"—i.e., existentially, experientially tuned in, ritually functional—has been overwhelmed. It has been muted if not crushed altogether. We do not trust ourselves to inhabit a rite as though it could speak for itself, the experience itself embodying its meaning. It was not always so. The resulting loss is a cultural development, not inevitable, but a predictable outcome of our own specific cultural history.

In his last meal with his disciples, Jesus distributed bread and cup and directed them to "*Do* this" for his remembrance. He did not say, "Explain this . . ." Nor did he say, "Reason this out," or "Debate this." One language of worship, often neglected in many churches, is body language. Movement, gesture, posture, action, touching, washing, anointing, eating and drinking, are all ways of expressing faith, praying for it, and simply engaging in bodily-present relationship with God and one another. Such action can be an experience in and of itself, not requiring any explanation—at least, not in the moment (please!). Insofar as we have reduced our body language to a minimum—sitting, standing, closing eyes—we impoverish ourselves and deprive ourselves of some kinds of "knowing" to which a more bodily and holistic engagement can serve as an opening.

We have muted, marginalized that other, precognitive sense of "knowing," which is sacramental experience, close-at-hand exposure to that which overflows the narrowly rational and the reductively logical. Today, to compensate for this loss, everything must be explained, and the explanation becomes more important than the experience, of which we have, sadly, learned to be suspicious. In order to be explained well enough to overcome our incapacitated intuitive senses, the explanation requires complexity. And complexity is difficult and easily dismissed or resisted and, frankly, it can end up being elitist. But, this situation is not hopeless. The way forward is to free ourselves to sing, bow and bend, pray, wash, anoint, and eat and drink our way through this culturally induced obstacle course.

5

Love

All you need is love, sweet love!
—LIONEL RICHIE

If Only . . .

THE PASTOR OR TEACHER who draws attention to doctrine or theology may encounter the objection of someone who dares to say what others may think but not say out loud. "All that stuff just gets in the way. What it's all about is love. Love is all we need. We don't need the Bible, or creeds, or 'organized religion.' We don't need faith. We just need to buckle down and love our neighbor. That's all the 'religion' we need." A sentiment not too surprising in an era in which many are repelled by what seems to be aggressive and ungenerous behavior hiding behind one theology or another—Islamic, yes, here and there; and even Jewish, sometimes; but nearer at hand and often, political/ideological evangelicalism; while none of us, of course, is entirely innocent.

Even among church people, some who have become disillusioned and disheartened by what seems to be the twilight of faith or the confusion that accompanies it will opine that we can just as easily get along without any theological or doctrinal reflection. Well-meaning folks sometimes offer the observation that, "If only everybody would just love one another, everything would be okay." True, that. But everybody does not "just love one another," and they never have, and it is reasonable to believe that they never will. Christian theology reflects on why that is the case, and in the process can save us from kidding ourselves. So, maybe there is good reason for theological reflection, after all. Why does love so often elude us?

For one thing, although love sounds simple, it isn't. Even for those whose resolve is to love, it is not always apparent what the loving thing to do might be in a particular situation. Take, for example an unplanned pregnancy. Imagine any imaginable scenario possible to describe the pregnant woman. Is she perhaps fourteen, pregnant by a member of her family? Or twenty-two years old, suffering with diabetes. She has a child at home, is working two part time jobs, has been abandoned by the baby's father and has no family to turn to for help. What would be the most loving counsel one might offer her? And, if love requires weighing separate interests of the prospective mother and the nascent life within her, how should that love be divided? The answers may seem simple for those who have already made up their minds, whether wearing labels marked pro-choice or pro-life. But the most loving answer will not be obvious to everybody, no matter how sensible and earnest. "If only everybody would just love one another . . ."

Or, you are a parent whose child has gotten into trouble repeatedly since high school, each offense escalating to a worse one. Drugs, petty thefts, indebtedness, and lost jobs led to homelessness. On each occasion, you came to the rescue, posting bail, finding and paying for rehab, reimbursing victims, intervening with acquaintances to find jobs, and providing shelter. Do you think the loving thing to do is to continue in these rescue operations? Or might it be to let your dearly loved offspring face the music in hopes of finding the inner resources to take responsibility for her own life? What is the most loving thing to do? The answer is not likely to be the same for every similar situation.

It may be that you are in a position to influence the setting of public policy. Government budgets are stressed. People resist raising taxes. But there are a number of individuals and families who, although they work for pay, have an income insufficient for basic needs. Do you use your influence to argue for an increase in the state or federal budget to help the disabled poor, the working poor, and their children buy food for their tables? Or provide subsidies for shelter? And what if some other budget item should have to be reduced—say, bridge maintenance, or emergency aid for victims of floods? Or maybe taxes should be raised enough to do all these things, whatever the circumstances, even if an increase works a hardship for those on fixed incomes. How should such a quandary be decided if we were truly committed to "just loving each other"? Or, is loving only for church people and others with altruistic sensibilities, with government permitted to turn a cold shoulder to selective groups of its own citizens without responsibility or fear of reproach?

I Do not Understand My Own Actions

Knowing what love requires in specific situations, whether in the affairs of a family or in setting public policy, is difficult, and it is not always easy to reach a consensus about it even among well-meaning people. But, beyond that, even when one has a clear idea of what love may require, the harder thing is to find the strength and energy to follow through. If love is so obviously the answer to everything, why is it so hard to do?

The traditional (orthodox) theological view is derived from both the Bible and experience. The apostle Paul summed it up.

> I do not understand my own actions. For I do not do what I want, but I do the very thing I hate . . . I can will what is right, but I cannot do it. For I do not do the good I want, but the evil I do not want is what I do. (Rom 7:15b, 19)

If one is honest, it is easy to recognize that Paul reflects experience common to all of us. Even should it be crystal clear what is right, and good, and loving, one often finds it impossible to do as one knows one ought.

Of course, Americans in particular are optimistic in temperament, and we prefer to believe that everybody really could do the right thing, the loving thing, if they only knew what it was. Without being aware of it, our fellow citizens are taking the side of Pelagius, a British monk who lived from 360–418 CE. Pelagius argued that human beings have free will, and can do what is right so long as they know what it is. His views were contested in particular by Augustine (354–430 CE). The controversy was addressed by the Council of Ephesus (431 CE), which decided to declare Pelagianism to be a heresy. The Reformers, including Luther and Calvin, went with Augustine and the Council.

Protestants in the twenty-first century are not much inclined to talk of heresy, but the fact of the matter is that modern psychology, while not arguing from a theological position, is not likely to agree with Pelagius that human beings have an entirely free will. It is not that God has programmed us in advance, subverting our freedom. But our freedom is constrained, in part because of the abundance of possible choices before which we rightly hesitate.

Our judgments and actions are shaped by many influences, of which we are often unaware. When faced with a decision, we have a sense that we might make a free choice to go one way or another, but in fact, while not actually pre-determined, we make choices under the influence of genes, personal experience both conscious and unconscious, and the many formal and informal communities of which we are a part or to whose values we have been exposed. We choose under the weight of personal and tribal interests that may not register consciously. "I do not understand my own actions. For I do not do what I want, but do the very thing I hate." This is an assessment of our own predicament that is too often made obvious only in retrospect.

If it were actually the case that all the world needs is for human beings to love each other, then it would seem as though all we would need would be . . . what? . . . some good advice? Such as a parent's counsel to a young child: "Don't steal your sister's cookie!" "Share your doll with your friend!" "Say 'thank you'!" Such admonitions, and the penalties that may serve to reinforce them, will probably not feel "loving" from the child's point of view. At least, not in the short run. But the child can learn to follow such rules, and ought to, because rules prove useful in minimizing conflict. But following the rules and loving one another are two different things. Children mature, they internalize the simplest rules, and then are expected to learn some that are more complex. The advice and counsel a parent offers to a child is mirrored in far more sophisticated versions from various sources suitable for adults. These may come from sages, ancient wisdom traditions, all the major world religions, popularizers like Benjamin Franklin, or even whoever writes the texts for greeting cards. This sort of advice is often quotable and memorable, and may indeed be useful.

Once learned, this practical wisdom can rein in some of our thoughtless impulses, help to keep the peace, and inspire generosity. To a point. Because another learning that begins in childhood but becomes more sophisticated as we age is the skill of rationalizing. We learn how to justify ourselves, our choices, and our actions. It is possible to develop the skill of rationalizing to a fine point: stealing isn't really stealing in this case, because . . . Cheating a customer isn't really cheating because . . . Not paying Social Security taxes on my employee (paying under the table) is justifiable because . . . Selling payday loans at inflated interest rates that multiply quickly is justifiable because . . .

Rationalizing

Rationalizing—self-justification—is a useful tool, always at hand. Even the best impulses may become distorted to the point that we do harm even when we neither intend it nor recognize it. For example, it is both natural and healthy and part of a good creation that we should want to be physically secure, to have enough food to eat, shelter for ourselves and those we love, as well as the attention and respect of others. It is natural and reasonable that we should want to store away resources we may not need now, but expect to need later for our future security. Nothing wrong with that. It is also natural and healthy to love one's own people—the folks most like us who share our nationality, our ethnic culture, our tastes, our circumstances, our politics, our faith. But there seems to be no internal governor that turns off our neediness, personal or corporate, when we have acquired enough. In fact, the more successful we are at gathering an adequate supply, it is often the case that the longing for more simply intensifies. Remember the bumper sticker? "Whoever ends up with the most toys wins!"

When the quite natural impulse to provide those things legitimately needed and desirable becomes swollen out of bounds; when our sense of bottomless neediness leads to outmaneuvering others, indifferent to their vital interests, then love does not appear to be part of the calculus. In fact, suspicion and hate flourish under those circumstances. Conflict, on a small or large scale, becomes inevitable. And the fact is that there is no human being who is entirely immune from the calculus of thinking of oneself (or one's family, or one's tribe) at the expense of others. "All have sinned and fall short of the glory of God . . ." (Rom 3:23).

Deep reflection on these matters, funded by scriptural narratives that offer profound insights into the human condition, has led to the Christian doctrine of sin—an unpopular word, often trivialized. But it is not a trivial matter. Sin is a kind of blindness, a self-deception that afflicts everyone in varying degrees. It manifests itself not just in personal moral and ethical indifference or power plays, but also in distortions to which groups and whole societies are vulnerable. In some of its more grotesque manifestations, sin metastasizes into phenomena for which "evil" is the only description that comes close to adequate.

"If only everybody would just love one another, everything would be okay." Indeed. But it has not ever happened. It is not happening now. And it will not happen, ever, in the world as we know it, short of the *basileia*. Why? Because even taking account of the multitude that is "everybody," and the unlikelihood that "everybody" will ever agree about what love requires and coordinate their efforts effectively, we may do harm even when our intentions are good. I see your problem; I know how to "fix" it; you become my project. In other words, impulses planted in the human race that are inherently good become distorted, twisted out of shape. None of us escapes from it. Our problem, as human beings, is not that we are inherently bad people. We are, more often than not, good enough people caught in patterns from which we are helpless to free ourselves. We are not short of wise counsel. All the good advice we should ever need is already in circulation.

The problem is that even the best advice serves only as a kind of band-aid ameliorating a problem that runs much deeper, lying within our very being. Why should it be so? We cannot say. We are all caught in a systemic brokenness, some untamable power of distortion that infects human beings singly and collectively, and holds us prisoner. The Bible does not try to explain it, but neither does it hesitate to name it, necessarily resorting to "Satan" or the evil one, shadowy personifications of the brokenness. All we can reasonably say is that even impulses meant for good can lead to bad outcomes. This is not pessimism. It is a realistic acknowledgment of the human dilemma. We are not in a position to save ourselves, even when well supplied with good advice. Fortunately, that is not the last word!

Is God Loving?

Human love may be fierce, but it turns out to be selective, and our insecurity easily turns good intentions into something else. The only love that is reliable is that which is rooted in the God whose love is stubborn; neither narrow or intimidated. The gospel tells us that God's love is where we need to rest our hope.

In our society, even atheists believe that the God they don't believe in is a loving God. To say that God loves, and that God's love is so reliable that it is not capable of being discouraged is to make a theological statement. But why *this* theological statement? That God loves, relentlessly? Why this? "Love" and "God" are not logically required to go together. In some cultures and some religious traditions, "love" is not a word normally associated with deity. Certainly they were not associated with one another in the common religious culture of the Mediterranean basin in the first century of the Common Era.

It was the gospel that introduced the conviction that God's disposition towards the human race and the world itself must be described as "loving." Christianity gets credit (or blame) for successfully imprinting such a view of God on the larger culture. That image of the divine has become, for the most part, the default setting in Western civilization, not only for Christians, but also for those who have no interest in any god at all. Our secular society may have no use for god-talk, but if there should be any talk of God, whether affirming or rejecting, it is of One who is simply taken for granted to be describable as loving. Therein lies a problem. Because, of course, along with the premise that God is loving goes the implication that if things do not go well for us—if that love should not be evident in a way that matches our expectations—it is God who must be at fault. The One said to be loving has obviously fallen down on the job. We shall punish this disappointing God with our unbelief! Of course, to declare that such a God does not exist is itself a theological statement that can be argued reasonably even if not definitively proved.

Why should we choose one of these theological statements over the other? That God is loving? or that God does not exist? The Christian gospel is not the product of a reasoned argument, speculating that there must be a God, and that this God might reasonably be expected to be loving. We make these affirmations in response to what we perceive to be God's self-revelation in Israel and in Jesus Christ.

Israel's narrative, recorded in our Old Testament, tells the story of the God identified to Moses only in the most basic of terms: "I AM" (Exod 3:14). It may be reasonable to believe that in human beings, evolutionary processes have led to creatures with consciousness, capable of self-examination, of seeing ourselves from something like an impartial observer's point of view. And, it may also be reasonable to presume that consciousness of that sort in sentient beings (us and perhaps creatures like us elsewhere in the universe) is not likely to have surfaced unless there is a greater consciousness at the very heart of things: "I AM." Reasonable, yes, although not provable—and not the source of the gospel's affirmations.

Israel's own historical experience was the unfolding of a series of liberating moves that turned the impossible into the possible.

- liberation from bondage in Egypt, against the wishes of the highest Egyptian authorities

- the gift of a geographical place in which they could grow into their identity as a people with a God-directed and universal mission

- a supply of prophetic voices that risked messages critical of their own people and institutions rather than only the crimes of their enemies

- disasters that served to highlight the perils that accompany complacent toleration of injustices and prideful presumptions of invulnerability.

- catastrophes that closed some historical chapters and opened others.

Israel was neither argued nor reasoned into a relationship (sometimes adversarial) with God. The relationship was simply embedded in their experience and their reflection on it. A word like "loving" is one that can, in retrospect, rightly describe the God whose identity and disposition were discerned to be at work in Israel's history.

Which is not to say that people in Israel were not puzzled, even angry, when God seemed to have deserted them. And yet, their disappointment and anger did not inevitably lead to denying God's existence. More typically, they simply felt free to take their anger and resentment directly to God.

> I say to God, my rock,
> "Why have you forgotten me?
> Why must I walk about mournfully
>   because the enemy oppresses me?"
> As with a deadly wound in my body,
>   my adversaries taunt me,
> while they say to me continually,
> "Where is your God?" (Ps 42:9–10)

Love Made Visible

For Christians, the narrative arc begun in Israel has become focused in a specific person, Jesus of Nazareth. In his story, a narrative specifically characterized by love becomes even clearer. His encounters with the sick, the outcast, the shunned, the poor, those abused by authority, as well as those who have themselves abused authority are marked by loving actions. Wherever he goes, his touch is a healing touch. The excluded are included, the unclean made clean, the sorrowful made glad, the emotionally distraught brought back to their right minds. The cruel and unjust wake up and fly right. The dead hear him call their names. Hell is emptied. A power of love of the truest sort is made manifest in Jesus, whose very person stirs deep questions.

One such question is, "By what authority are you doing these things, and who gave you this authority?" (Matt 21:23). The testimony of the gospel is that it is God's own authority that has become personally manifest in the person of Jesus. His acts of compassion represent God's disposition towards us, and a promise that the ultimate destiny of the world will be a new creation, one freed from the brokenness that shatters so many lives. That new creation will be characterized by the kind of transformation that flowed from Jesus wherever he went, and of which his resurrection is an example, a promise and a down payment.

You can have Confucianism without Confucius; but you cannot have Christianity without Jesus Christ. Confucianism is a system of philosophical observations meant to guide and interpret life. Those who follow it may or may not have any interest in Confucius. What he taught matters. Who he was does not.

In the case of Christianity, Jesus is not dispensable. His person is the content of the faith—not just his teaching. First and foremost, he embodies the presence of God incarnated into our conflicted humanity. In his acts we recognize acts of God. In retrospect we discern his authority as implementing the authority of God. In his itinerant ministry in Galilee and Judea, he made visible God's character and disposition towards us. He is the living definition of God as love. Those who knew him and gathered around him could speak confidently of God's loving character because they believed they had encountered it in the person of Jesus. The power of that love is manifest in his life, death and resurrection, in which God in Christ directly challenges and overcomes both the personal and impersonal forces of death and destruction. As his disciples told his story and shared his influence across the formidable boundaries of the world, they made available to people of whatever ethnicity a new and entirely unconventional way of thinking and speaking of God.

A philosophy—any system of thought—can influence the mind, and, through the mind, shape perceptions of reality and guide behavior. It may or may not touch the whole person—heart and soul as well as the mind. The most penetrating influence comes when heart, soul, and mind are all engaged in concert. This requires a disposition that has traditionally been labeled "piety."

A Piety Shaped by Love

We don't much like the word "piety," because "pious" is most familiar these days as a term of derision, but if you are able to disassociate it with a sense of smug superiority and hypocritical pretension, it might still be serviceable. Piety at its best is a discipline of reverent devotion. In Christian faith, the object of reverent devotion is Jesus, the human face and heart of God. Without piety—disciplined, reverent devotion—the gospel becomes a system of ideas that may or may not withstand the tumbles and earthquakes of a lifetime. When life experiences challenge ideas, the ideas may be given up. Piety is more likely to persevere even when we are shaken. We may argue with God, shake a fist at God, threaten to withdraw our faith in God, and piety permits it and coexists with it.

Christian piety is expressed not only in personal habits and common worship, but also in one's personal and communally shared engagement with our environment, including the non-human environment. It has an effect on how we conduct our lives, personally and politically. It is shaped, at best, when it is a piety that is enabled to imagine a world that looks like the one we glimpse in the story of Jesus and in his promise of a new creation. That is, a world in which God invites us to join in the effort to make people and things whole. A world in which we do not permit ourselves to be indifferent to brokenness, injuries, injustices, and deliberate distortions that seek to rationalize and hide these things. A crucial role of the church in cultivating this kind of piety is to continue to hold before our eyes Jesus and the transformations he enabled, experienced, and promised. That includes calling ourselves out, in a prophetic voice, when we discover acts of deception and self-deception, or consent to them. "Loving" might be an appropriate shorthand label with which to describe this kind of piety, but it is not the sentimental kind of love that presumes we can generate it in adequate measure all by ourselves. "If only everybody would just . . . "

Rather, it is an eyes-open, realistic sort of love, tamed by our constant need to repent for the many ways we misuse it, misrepresent it, and exercise it in ways that do harm, however unintentionally. If the world is to be saved, it will be God who saves it. And it is just such a divine commitment that we have seen in Jesus. Our role is significant, but it is a supporting one. God, in God's own way, calls us to be useful, employing our hopes, prayers, energies, and strategies to be harmonized with God's own saving action, as far as God may enable it.

And it is indeed God who enables us. Human beings, broken as we are, have nevertheless been made in the image of God. As such, we are capable of altruism, of selfless action on behalf of others, of true empathy that extends beyond self, family, and tribe. These things we undertake to do, sometimes spontaneously, sometimes by disciplining ourselves to do it, often in concert with others, and always, consciously or not, as instruments of the love that flows from God, the ultimate source of all love.

The early Christians were accused of being atheists, because they refused to acknowledge Caesar as Lord. Indeed, they were atheists in more ways than that, and are still today. Ecumenical Christians are likely to be atheists with respect to any god who favors one race, gender, ethnicity, nationality, or economic class over the others. We are atheists with respect to any god whose intention and delight is to spy out occasions to punish for punishment's sake. We are atheists with respect to any god who is indifferent to people's pain or to injustice. We are atheists with respect to any god who merely observes the world at a distance, indifferently, and absent of any long-run purpose. We are atheists with respect to the many homemade gods manufactured by the culture to stir up resentments, envy, and tribalism. We are atheists with respect to any human being, party, ideology, scheme, or system that claims absolute authority, just as we rejected Caesar's absolutist claims in the first century. To the extent that we are atheists in these respects, we honor and embrace the God about whom we could say little or nothing apart from what we have seen in Jesus Christ.

In Christ, we have a picture of God engraved upon our hearts. And the God whose picture we have in Christ is a God who loves "the world." Not just a few people in the world. Not just those who have it all figured out. But God loves the reckless, the cocksure, those wracked with doubt, the unbelievers, the timid, the indifferent—the crucified, and even the crucifiers.

Cross-shaped Love

Of course, Jesus was crucified, wasn't he. It seems unusual, to say the least, that an entire devotional community should have been formed around someone who was a victim of capital punishment. Particularly so when, in his own culture, death by crucifixion was considered to signal that the victim was cursed. "[F]or anyone hung on a tree is under God's curse" (Deut 21:23).

It is relatively easy, in some quarters of mainline Protestantism, to bypass all the cross-stuff, the gory stuff, the unspiritual stuff. After all, we can always talk about love without getting bogged down with the cross. What difference does it make how Jesus died? Isn't it really all about how he lived? What he taught?

Here, it may be, is the crux of it: Jesus was what he taught. And he taught what he was. He taught that the godforsaken mattered to God. And he was numbered among the godforsaken. In other words, God in Christ became one of the godforsaken. God has joined and still joins us in all the many cross-shaped places of the world.

We might imagine that an all-powerful God might do better simply to eliminate the possibility of cross-shaped places. Seems like a worthy proposal, but it does not describe our experience. If we try to explain horrors, or make sense of them, we will be undertaking a fool's errand. Evil and suffering are beyond rationality and cannot and ought not be construed as serving some useful purpose. All that we can say, trusting in the gospel, is that God knows godforsakenness from the inside and shares it, and, in fact, despises it.

If we focus on Jesus' teaching, we will find these words: "If any want to be my followers, let them deny themselves and take up their cross and follow me" (Mark 8:34). This is not commending martyrdom. It is an invitation to join the team of the vulnerable. It does not suggest that suffering for its own sake wins some kind of merit badge. Those who work up the courage to follow him—one step at a time, one by one and together—take up the challenge of the risky love that crosses boundaries. That includes the excluded. Sees the value of those who have not been valued. Shares good things with those who have nothing to give in return. And, like the One on the cross, that kind of love doesn't count up grievances, doesn't pass along injuries; doesn't try to get even. And sooner or later, that means some kind of hurt. Mostly small hurts. Sometimes big ones.

Some forms of spirituality warn us away from love of any kind. We may be urged, as a spiritual discipline, to work towards detachment. Don't get involved and you're less likely to get hurt. Disengagement is a struggle to minimize one's own suffering, the kind that accompanies inevitable losses. For those who manage to achieve serious detachment, when good deeds go unnoticed or disappointments wear us down; when a loss threatens to overwhelm us, or the sorrows of the world make us sad, the resulting hurt might get sealed off. Training ourselves not to care may seem like a burden lifted.

Jesus beckons us to walk in a different direction. "For those who want to save their life"—that is, those whose aim is to wall themselves off from the downside that accompanies emotional investment in others—"will lose it; and those who lose their life for my sake, and for the sake of the gospel"—that is, those who risk becoming vulnerable—"will save it" (Mark 8:35). Such is the paradox. "Losing" is transformed into "saving"—a calculus written on the very heart of God.

The heart of the Christian gospel is, I believe, vulnerability. Not a search for spiritual ecstasies, not even an undisturbed peace cultivated in an inwardly focused Christian life. Jesus on the cross—as well as the Jesus taking risks for strangers and the Jesus who teaches us how and where to take up our own crosses—is marked by his vulnerability. And he invites us to take the risks of vulnerability, one by one and shared with the whole church. It is true that love is all we need. But it is love of the sort made manifest in Jesus on his cross. A love that has already written the future he has enabled us to imagine. This love does not look like chest-thumping braggadocio as though we could save the world on our own by sheer willpower, energy, or determination, but looks like vulnerability. In being open to the stranger; in sharing, in some measure, the hurts of the wounded. Such vulnerability is not careless or reckless, but a conviction that, in God's calculus, there is enough love to cover many losses.

Faith helps us to find the courage to imagine, to discern, to see the deep foundations God has laid to support a way of being in the world. The deepest of those foundations is God's love made manifest in cross and resurrection—the only love that has the power of consistency and the ability to effect true transformation. The work of theology—doctrine—is to bring clarity to such matters. Love is indeed all we need. But the love we need is a different love than the "If only everybody . . ." kind.

6

Language Lessons

Tell all the truth but tell it slant.
—EMILY DICKINSON

We Are All Literalists

THE LANGUAGE THAT MOST faithfully and most fulsomely embodies the Christian faith is the language of Scripture. In other eras, most people were familiar enough with Scripture that they could be expected to navigate its several languages intuitively. They might be able to find their way easily enough among proverbs, parables, narratives, similes, and metaphors, even if they did not know those technical words. That is less often the case today. To add to the difficulty, fundamentalism and Enlightenment rationalism, an odd couple, have succeeded in persuading the general public, even those who are not fundamentalists themselves, that the language of the Bible is to be read, no matter what the genre, with the same literalistic expectations we bring to a science or history text.

This sort of literalism, equivalent or nearly equivalent to fundamentalism, treats Scripture not as witness to the Word of God, but as though it were a transcription of words (plural) proceeding directly from the mouth of God. This sort of literalism approaches the Bible as though we are to believe in Christ because we first believed in the authority of Scripture, instead of the other way around. The right way around is to acknowledge and honor the Bible's authority because Scripture has taken us by the hand and led us to Jesus Christ, the Word of God incarnate, to whom it witnesses. The Bible, as witness to Jesus, uses language in a variety of ways to introduce us to him as our mentor and refuge.

Gordon Lathrop notes that "we belong to a literal time, unused to rich metaphoric speech . . . a time of an often murderous religious literalism . . ."[1] Even so-called "progressives" are inclined to a certain kind of literalism. One can sometimes find examples in biblical commentaries by scholars who would certainly deny being literalists. For example, a kind of literalist reading of the feeding of the multitudes[2] could include the speculative judgment that the real "miracle" was that someone in the crowd might have taken the initiative to share a bit of bread or fish. Moved by the generosity of that one person, others in the crowd presumably became inspired to share from their own private supplies. Should that have been the case, the biblical account of an unexpected abundance of food may be judged believable in a literal sense just by offering an explanation where the Gospel writers had chosen to keep silent. Perhaps the Gospels have piously framed the story, holding back some details in such a way as to magnify the reputation of the central figure? That is one way that a moralizing, de-theologized version, the presumably "real" story, becomes the preferred and authoritative version of it. If we accept that, we are saved from having to stretch our imagination to accommodate something significantly out of the ordinary; or, at least saved from perceiving whatever extraordinary thing the Gospel writer is trying to show us. The end product is a literalism resting on conjecture. It "saves" the text for twenty-first-century readers while missing the point.

When one looks at the story more carefully, with the larger biblical context in mind, it becomes clear enough that the point was to serve a basically theological purpose. Old Testament parallels offer a clue to apprehending the story more deeply. For example, one obvious precedent to the feeding of the multitudes is the story of the prophet Elisha feeding a hundred people when only a small supply of food was available. Onlookers were certain that the food on hand would not be enough. But, "He set it before them, they ate and had some left . . ." (2 Kgs 4:42–44). The Gospels interpret Jesus feeding the multitudes by making a subtle but intentional comparison with the prophet Elisha.[3]

1. Lathrop, *Saving Images*, 23, 24.
2. Matt 14:13–21; Mark 6:30–44; Luke 9:10–17; John 6:1–13.
3. A similar story of food supplies not running out is told about the prophet Elijah,

Matthew and Mark frame the story as one taking place in "a deserted place," more literally, in the original Greek, a "wilderness place" (Matt 14:15, Mark 6:31). Their intention is to call to mind Israel's exodus experience in the wilderness (Exod 16:1), when God answered the hungry people's complaint by directing Moses to tell them that food would be provided: manna, "bread from heaven" (Exod 16:4). The Gospels are sending a broad signal that Jesus stands in a succession that includes Moses as well as the prophets Elijah and Elisha, the authority of both the Law and the Prophets being united in him.

A third parallel is drawn from Psalm 23. For example, Jesus told his disciples "to get all the people to sit down in groups on the green grass" (Mark 6:39). To mention that the grass was green seems a curious detail until we recall the psalmist's "He makes me lie down in green pastures" (Ps 23:1). Further, Jesus has compassion for the hungry crowds, "because they are like sheep without a shepherd" (Mark 6:34). Pointing out the people's need for one like a shepherd recalls the prophet Zechariah, who had voiced the same lament that Ezekiel and others had made, "Therefore the people wander like sheep; they suffer for lack of a shepherd" (Zech 10:2). In Mark's version of the story, the only one that makes explicit the "shepherd" reference, it points to Jesus as the longed-for shepherd, which is particularly striking since the original Hebrew of Psalm 23 is "YHWH[4] is my shepherd."

It is no coincidence, either, that the feeding action describes Jesus using a sequence of four verbs, variants of *took* a loaf of bread, *blessed* (or gave thanks), *broke*, and *gave* the bread. This is the same four-word sequence that appears in the stories of the Last Supper, as well as the story of the risen Lord at table with two disciples on the road to Emmaus (Luke 24:30).[5] It is reminiscent of Jesus presiding over a eucharistic meal, with the disciples, who distributed the food, taking the role of deacons or communion ministers. Note also the climax of the story: "And all ate and were filled," reminiscent of both the Elijah and Elisha stories and, in Ps 23:5, "You prepare a table before me; my cup overflows." There is, in each case, more than enough.

---

predecessor of Elisha, and the widow of Zarephath (1 Kgs 17:7–16).

4. YHWH is the holy name of God, normally not spoken.

5. Last Supper narratives: Matt 26:26; Mark 14:22; Luke 22:19. A slight variation of the words in John 6:11.

Literalism May Narrow Our Vision

It is not possible to find our way behind the Gospel narratives to investigate what "really" happened, but it is evident that the feeding stories intend to evoke resonances intended to help us to discern Jesus' identity and role. God's hand is meant to be visible in the story as the Gospel writers perceived it. Theirs is not simply an indifferent snapshot of a moment in Jesus' ministry, but testimony to the glory of God made manifest in Jesus presiding over a meal for people who are hungry both physically and spiritually. The feeding story is one more example of how the *basileia*[6] is made tangibly manifest in a specific moment. It is a preview and down payment on the promised renewal of all things, the ultimate future, as imagined, for example, in the image of the wedding supper of the Lamb (Rev 19:9).

The underlying presumption of the kind of biblical literalism that rests on historical conjecture is that the meaning of the event can only be determined if we have access to an accurate picture of the historical moment as it would have appeared to an attentive, objective, and critical observer. Get the history right, and you will get the meaning of the story right. Right? If that should be the case, the challenge would always be to try to look *behind* a difficult text using whatever tools and speculative possibilities might be available to help us sniff out the presumed *real* story. The goal would be to come up with a plausible picture of what might "really" have happened, presuming that the story as told needs to be corrected. A "plausible" picture means one that is acceptable as measured by the standards of our own culture. After all, it is usually possible to hypothesize an every day kind of explanation for anything that stretches beyond the bounds of the ordinary, as numerous biblical commentators and some preaching ministers have demonstrated.

Another way of looking at it, however, is to accept the possibility that the event itself, even if it could be successfully reconstructed by a skillful student, might not in fact transparently reveal its meaning. Even if a prize-winning journalist had been present, she might have seen without seeing. Even if the story should rest on a literal "miracle of sharing," the vital center of the story might easily be missed should one be blind or indifferent to the trail of clues laid by the Gospel writers. What the Gospel writer sees is not necessarily the same as what the journalist might see. The Gospel

---

6. *Basileia* is the Greek New Testament word for the kingdom/reign/dominion of God, the culmination of God's redemptive work.

writer is not merely describing a curious scene to be reported offhandedly. Any recalled event requires that the person reporting it engage in an act of interpretation. Just to put it into a form that can be told is to interpret it, even when one tries to keep an objective distance. There is no doubt that the Gospel writers were interpreters who, in good conscience, served another purpose than journalistic detachment. Their engagement with the story and its central figure evoked communal memories that helped them to see what otherwise they might not have seen. Scriptural antecedents and their own experience of the church's sacramental meal helped them to look back retrospectively on the feedings of the multitudes from a different perspective than that of a dispassionate observer.

The Gospel writers' task, as they see it, is to construct a theological statement; i.e., to help the reader to discern how the event is to be received by those reflecting on it. They do it by means of their interpretive narratives. A hypothetical historical reconstruction of the scene might easily trivialize it. The more authentic vision is given in the theological insight of the primary interpreter. The interpreter helps the reader to see what might be missed were the story to be told otherwise. The Gospel writer uses verbal images as an artist might use graphic ones, trying to capture the essence of a narrated event when the essence may not be immediately obvious on the surface.

As for the church, its experience has been to hear a word from God in the story as understood and shared by Matthew, Mark, Luke, or John. Not relying on a hypothetical reconstruction, but in the event as it was theologically interpreted and narrated in the actual texts of the Gospels. For faith, it is not a matter of being pressed to make an intellectual decision about exactly what happened and how, but rather of recognizing and embracing the Jesus made manifest in and by the text: the Jesus who invites us all to the ultimate welcome table. He who takes, blesses, breaks and gives the loaf is himself, so to speak, "the bread of life," "the bread that came down from heaven," "bread to strengthen the human heart" (Mark 6:35, 6:41; Ps 104:15). This heavenly bread will not run short. The meaning of the story is sufficiently clear. Whether its essential message is true is another thing. It is quite possible to get what the Gospel writer intended to say, but not believe it; but, in faith, it is possible both to understand it and to cherish it.

Same Words, Two Languages

To speak or write in the language appropriate to science, history, journalism, or technology requires a kind of grammar that serves well enough the presumption of one kind of literalism or another. But it is handicapped when it comes to recognizing a real, but entirely different dimension of interpreting and communicating experience. The general culture has persuaded us all to presume that even matters of faith need to be framed in something at least resembling scientific, historically objective discourse. However, to grasp what biblical language does, one needs to rise to the challenge of assuming a modestly counter-cultural stance. In other words, not to read Scripture through the eyes either of the fundamentalist or the religious skeptic, both of whom tend to read it alike, although for different purposes. How might one bear witness to instances that highlight the extraordinary grace of God made manifest in unexpected ways when the only tool at hand is practical, utilitarian language? The counter-cultural challenge is to appreciate how familiar words can be used to serve a purpose different from the one intended by the writer of textbooks. Language can serve to channel an experience, to create a kind of meeting place, just as it can also be used to shape the intellect. A poet knows the difference.

A published poet has been invited to read some of her poems in a local bookstore. After reading one, a member of the audience raises a hand and asks, "But what does it mean?" The poet pauses, is puzzled. Then she reads the poem again. What? Why?

She reads the poem again because what it means is part and parcel of the poetic form itself. The rhythm, the beat of the language; the way the words play against each other; the choice of repeated sounds and echoed phrases—however the poet has shaped the work, its meaning is something to be encountered and inhabited in the course of reading it and hearing it read. What one feels/experiences/intuits as it is read *is* what it means. Of course, it is possible for a communication failure to occur whatever the language used. A failure to understand the poem might be the result of a failure of the poet's effort; or of a premature effort to decode the "meaning" as though hearing the poem once should be sufficient to grasp its meaning instantly and effortlessly; or caused by a misplaced expectation that the poem intends to use language the same way a textbook does.

The fact is that most of us would probably feel inclined to ask the same question as the impatient member of the poet's audience: "What does it mean?" The question is, in effect, a request that the poet state the meaning in straightforward, analytic, scientific/journalistic, explanatory language—the only language we associate with the explication of "meaning." But language is a supple thing. As Emily Dickinson understood, there are times when the only way to communicate the truth successfully is to tell it *slant*. In other words, to find ways to make language work for you by making extraordinary use of the ordinary tools at hand.

It may be that students in a local English class will be starting a unit on poetry. A teacher who attended the reading at the bookstore will assign the poem. The students (those who did their homework!) will, of course, ask their teacher what it means. A discussion will ensue. The teacher will read it out loud. He will draw their attention to the fact that there is a beat to the language. Count it out: *one*, two, three, four; *one* two three, four—accent falls on *one*. The teacher will point out how an adjective curiously used (or invented from scratch, a blend of two others) may give a new perspective on the noun it modifies. Another will read the poem aloud, and this time recurrent vowel sounds might be noticed. Someone will ask again, "But what does it mean?" Various others will try to explain what they think it "means," using ordinary language appropriate to a different universe of meaning than that embodied in the language-phenomenon of the poem. "It kind of echoes the rhythm of . . . what? a waterfall? a marching army? a heartbeat? a fall down the stairs?" And then they will try to discern what was in the poet's mind, what experience she was trying to evoke, how her technique served that purpose, and how she felt about it. They will "explain" it, yes, but quite differently from the way the poem "explains" itself.

Both the reading of the poem and the analytic class discussion have a legitimate place, but each uses language differently. The class discussion uses the literal, detached language most familiar to us when speaking of impersonal matters. It is an objective analysis, not requiring a personal emotional investment. It consists of facts to be discerned and correctly identified, even when the "facts" are characterizations of feelings. The reading in the bookstore, however, uses language as though the vessel of language itself manifests an experience, an intuitive encounter that is parallel to but different from analytic reasoning: *slant*.

The believer needs to learn both ways of using language and be able to move back and forth between them. It is not so much a case of translating one language into another, but learning to pick up intuitively how to listen to each, sometimes with the help of the other. This is not a huge stretch, because we are already in the habit of moving between the language of a commercial transaction, for example, and the language of a popular song, or a hymn. We perceive differently the systematic language of the recipe for making macaroni and cheese and the lyrical language of a ballad. One is processed as a series of mechanical steps, the other is simply experienced, apprehended, inwardly processed at multiple levels. Language lessons, so to speak, are necessary because when we deal with serious matters—faith, for example—we find ourselves needing to overcome a culturally driven obstacle. The obstacle is that when it comes to faith, we imagine that we are meant to hear spoken or written language (e.g., sermon or Bible) as both the fundamentalists and skeptics do, as though we are speaking of God, Christ, Spirit in the same unequivocal language we use to explain compound interest.

Preaching as Sacramental Event

Preaching is necessarily an extension of biblical language, while at the same time it also makes use of language that provides information and/ or explains. The purpose of preaching has been understood differently at various times and places. In much of Protestantism, it has been understood non-sacramentally. By separating Word and Sacrament most of the time, the absence of Eucharist has contributed to what I believe to be a misunderstanding of preaching. When the sacrament that is meant to accompany, complement, open up, interpret and even critique the sermon is missing, the expectations for preaching become misshapen. Without the sacrament it is easy to gather the impression that preaching is a lecture on a religious topic; i.e., meant to provide either information or exhortation.

Preaching might best be understood as a sacramental event. While information may be given and exhortations made, a sacramental understanding of preaching is that in the sermon we expect to encounter the presence of God in the risen Christ. The people are drawn into that presence by the power of the Holy Spirit speaking in, through (and maybe in spite of) the sermon itself. While one might yearn for the sense of being in God's presence to be an extended one, it is often enough brief, even momentary. It is an instant in which the sermon itself—maybe a single word or a phrase—becomes an intersection, a spark of connection between God and the people, a meeting of spirits that bridges the distance between them. The sermon might be understood as analogous to the reading of the poem, described earlier. In the poem read aloud, the meaning is embedded in the action, the "doing" of it. An analytic discussion that follows may either open us to experience the liveliness of the poem, or suck the life out of it.

Yet the mechanics of a sermon's presentation will always call for a mixed medium, in the sense that information-giving will need to be interwoven with language that is told *slant*; that is, in ways congruent with the metaphorical, imaginative, precognitive, and intuitive. The juxtaposition with analytic, information-giving language can serve as a set of clues, a guide to acquiring the skills required to appreciate a language that is meant to do something different than only to supply information.

Does a biblical text describe what one might call a miracle—say, the parting of the sea during the exodus? Our first question is likely to be an analytic one, "Did it really happen?" A better question might be, "What purpose does this story serve?" It will not prove useful to look behind the story as though it were important to verify the historical details in order to make a judgment about whether it actually happened, or happened as described. The story, like the poem read aloud in the bookstore, is a narrative vehicle pressed into service to communicate a people's reading of their experience with the God to whom they attribute their liberation. The vehicle is not dispensable, any more than the experienced meaning of the poem could be made manifest apart from the actual poem. The "meaning" of the story of safely crossing the sea will not be perceived in the same way without engaging the story as it has been told.

Of course, it is nevertheless possible to examine the structure of the story, the history of its formation and the history of its interpretation in an analytic way appropriate to a classroom. No problem. But the analytic discussion cannot replace the story itself, because it serves a different purpose. The story is not a journalist's report, but a means to provide us experiential access to a people's celebration of an act of God. It is meant to communicate not just information about a moment in the past, but something of the wonder sparked by that specific moment however it may have unfolded: the awe, the impossible made possible, a way opened when there was no way, an immoveable obstacle removed, hopelessness turned into hope. If my analysis causes me to miss or intellectualize the wonder, then I will miss the celebration, and the celebration is the point, the purpose for which the story is remembered and told. The story is handed on not from a detached point of view, but existentially, from a deeply attached perspective, and its truest meaning can be experienced only from that perspective. The story was framed calling to mind a pivotal moment in a relationship between a people and the God perceived to have implemented a divine purpose for them, with them, and through them. Its meaning can only be experienced relationally. An inability to imagine and thus have access to wonder or awe, even though second-hand, means no celebration—and without celebration, no personal response, no embrace of the chief actor, no movement of the soul.

What about Easter?

And what about the resurrection of the Lord? Lots of people who otherwise seldom or never go to church may be found in pews on Easter Sunday. For many, their presence is a matter of deference to family or to custom. Many find themselves uncontrollably skeptical. And among all these may be found some who are hoping—hoping that faith might somehow spring up sufficient to overcome their skepticism.

"Is the resurrection a metaphor?" a young man asked the pastor. If the answer should be "Yes, it's a metaphor," one might take it to mean that it has more to do with an appealing idea than to do with the living God. Or, perhaps more to do with nature, new growth, and blossoms appearing where everything appeared—accent on the *appeared*—to be dead. If the answer given were to be "No, it's a literal fact," then it would seem that we are dealing with an historical occurrence that can be investigated, with the possibility of verification.

The resurrection does not fit either of those categories: metaphor, or the kind of fact that we are permitted to describe, too simply, as literal. And yet, in a sense, it is both. We are dealing here with an event—an actual happening of some kind, but something that cannot by any means be made to fit into any known category. In the twentieth chapter of John, the Gospel writer describes the risen Lord's appearance to the remaining disciples after the resurrection. When they had been hiding out in a locked room, Jesus appears among them, shockingly and unexpectedly. Thomas was not present at the time, and he was stunned when he heard the disciples' report of this visitation. One can imagine him wanting desperately to believe his colleagues' excited testimony while bracing himself for the most bitter of disappointments. (After a Friday's lesson in bitterly cruel disappointment.)

A week later, under similar circumstances, Jesus appears again, but this time Thomas is present. Even face-to-face, Thomas is not certain that he is seeing Jesus. Recognizing that the wary Thomas was not about to risk becoming victimized by a group hallucination or a cruel hoax, Jesus invited Thomas to touch him to identify the wounds suffered on the cross. John, telling this story, was testifying that the risen Lord was not a ghost, because ghosts are phantoms, and cannot be touched. But neither was he a resuscitated corpse, because resuscitated corpses cannot appear behind solid walls and locked doors. Not immediately recognized, Jesus was not just an unmarked continuation of the One whom Thomas and the others had been following in Galilee, Judea, and Samaria, as though his death had been nothing more than a brief interruption. In other words, the phenomenon of the resurrection was objectively real, indelibly imprinted on the souls of the astonished disciples; but there are no words adequate to describe it, categorize it, or do justice to it. We embrace the disciples' awkward testimony in spite of the fact that it presses up against the limits of what is humanly conceivable, much less scientifically describable.

The resurrection is not a dead body revived; nor a phantasmal spirit separated from a body. By an act of God, rather than by some natural process, Jesus in his real self and in the crisis of his death is who he has always been, but transformed. His resurrection serves God's purpose to signal that God is likely to be found in cross-shaped places but will not be overcome by them. God is strong enough to pull us out of the cross-shaped places, and neither death nor hell will have the last word. Even those whom society discards as abandoned, even cursed, have an Advocate who is stronger than death and the forces that deal in death. And, the risen Lord is God's signature on a promissory note for the renewal of the whole created order: a new creation, a new heaven and earth, to be similarly transformed by God's own power.

One can, of course, follow our natural and learned skepticism and deny it all, or reduce it to a metaphorical statement about possibilities for making a new start when it appears that all has been lost. Such a metaphorical statement would not be wrong, but it is certainly incomplete. The metaphor does not work apart from the act of God that justifies it: the specifically impossible made possible.

Like the claim that everything that is comes from God, the resurrection cannot be investigated, proved, or demonstrated. One receives it, if at all, in faith. That is, trusting that it is in accord with the character of the God revealed in Jesus Christ, in whom we glimpse God's disposition toward the human race and the whole creation. To receive it in faith requires that we employ capacities with which we have been born, but that the dominant culture has nearly programmed out of us; in fact, functionally disabled. Those are the capacities for imagining; i.e., "seeing" with the heart; for giving in to hope; i.e., "remembering" the future; and for trusting that some things that are not obvious can be truly discerned, even though they cannot be accessed via the scientific method. Lift up your hearts! The Lord is risen! He is risen indeed!

7

Mission

Mission is [the] church's acknowledgment
of the incompleteness of its own life."

—Amy Plantinga Pauw[1]

Crossing Boundaries

THE FIRST CHRISTIANS UNDERSTOOD themselves to be a community with a mission, although they would probably have phrased it differently. The mission is represented in the Gospel of Matthew when it recalls Jesus' authoritative mandate: "Go therefore and make disciples of all nations . . . baptizing . . . teaching . . ." (Matt 28:19–20). The scope of the mission was universal, and it crossed every conceivable boundary, beginning with the one that divided Jew from Gentile. It is also eschatological;[2] i.e., unlikely to be perfectly fulfilled short of the coming of the *basileia*.

On this (anticipatory) side of the *basileia*, the number of disciples will never reach 100 percent of the world's population, and maybe not on the other side either. At the bottom of "hell" there may be no one, but since there is no coercion in God's mission, it is conceivable that one who prefers to keep a distance from God might choose independence over reconciliation

---

1. Plantinga Pauw, *Church in Ordinary Time*, 155.

2. Eschatology refers to the phenomena related to the advent of God's ultimate future, the *basileia* (kingdom of God), when the divine rule will be fully realized; e.g., commonly, Christ's "second coming."

and never relent of the choice. We are not in a position to know how these matters will be resolved.

Realistically, it is nevertheless possible to see many boundaries as the artificial dividing points that they are. While respecting communal identities that exhibit a variety of rich possibilities, each different from the other, the Christian mission is broadly inclusive. It is not meant to be ethnically, racially, class, gender, or nationality based. It has been proved reasonable to presume that in every sort of community there will be those who find themselves drawn to Jesus Christ and his gospel. Reaching out to them began with Jesus, expanded outward from the first twelve and then the larger group around them, and the reaching out has never ceased. The church today does, in fact, include Christians from every continent, race, and ethnicity, to name only a few of the identifiers that tend to sort us by one category or another. On the other hand, it is more typical than not to find local congregations composed primarily of one race or socio-economic class. Technically, we are "catholic" in terms of overall inclusivity, but that catholicity is less visible up close.

A hundred years ago, "mission" was generally plural, "missions," and it most often referred to missionary work and other projects for which evangelism was foundational: spreading the gospel, church planting, making converts at home and abroad. The book of Acts provided a model. The apostle Paul, for example, made a public pitch for the gospel to the intellectually curious in the Athenian equivalent of Hyde Park (Acts 17:22–31). In other cases, he and others visited Jewish enclaves in various cities of the Roman Empire hoping to find an audience that could harbor persons who might be receptive and provide a sympathetic hearing (Acts 13:13–44).

In the U.S., the various "awakenings" as early as the eighteenth century, when the preacher George Whitefield preached to crowds, and the nineteenth-century mass evangelistic meetings led by Dwight Moody and Charles Finney; and Billy Graham's crusades as recently as the twentieth century are dramatic examples of public evangelism. In the twenty-first century, the method is more likely to be evangelism by television, radio, podcast, or social media.

For Everything There Is a Season

We have reached a moment, however, in which much speaking may be counter-productive. The gospel has always been much more than "God has a plan for your life," or a list of sequential steps to salvation to be ticked off one by one. The news media, that once upon a time used to be hands-off when it came to reporting church-related scandals, tiptoe around them no longer. We know about child sexual abuse, clerical misconduct of other sorts, and mega-church pastors or televangelists who have become fabulously wealthy on the backs of their flocks. Plenty of examples exist of Christians who invoke a certain kind of religious privilege, trying to purge textbooks for sectarian purposes, or impose prayers in neutral venues or subvert the science curricula or discredit sexual minorities or enact "religious freedom" laws at the expense of others. It seems not likely to be a receptive time for public preaching, whether to a crowd or even one on one. Not a good time for leaving tracts to be found in public restrooms, or handed out on the street or attached to doorknobs.

In and for the church, our speech needs to be clearer, more focused than ever; but in public places, we would do better, perhaps, to exercise our listening skills. Many Americans believe they already know all they will ever want to know about Christianity. They may not, in fact, know very much, but they are not in a mood to be enlightened about what they do not know. Fundamentalists and their near kin have taken center stage, and it is they who have succeeded in defining Christianity in the minds of the general public. Those who have accidentally happened upon radio preachers while searching for music on the dial discover, in thirty seconds, what they don't want to hear anything more about. So it is a time, in most instances, for the church to hone the skill of listening, studying how actually to hear the other. Let our speaking in matters of faith be discreet (not stealthy!), spare, modest, but available should a conversation partner signal a desire to hear from us.

In preaching the gospel in church the aim should be that the preacher recognize and take account of the current state of affairs, helping to support faith since it is constantly being challenged directly or indirectly by a culture that has, in large part, moved on. However, the service of worship is not intended to be a set-up in which the faithful appear and play their part in a crowd scene that has as its primary intention to evangelize the one (or one hundred) visitors who may walk in. The Lord's Day service and its many predecessors all the way back to the first century is not the front-line of an evangelistic or member-recruiting effort. When the service draws someone to Jesus Christ and his church, that is a happy side effect, not the purpose of the gathering.

So, how does the church communicate the gospel beyond its own walls? One way is through mission. Today expressed in the singular, the word "mission" tends to embrace a far broader palette of possibilities, including feeding the hungry, uniting with others to provide and support community efforts to protect from exploitation the poor and those who cannot look out for themselves; helping to build a Habitat house; providing legal support, advocacy, or hospitality for newcomers to this country; gathering winter coats for those without them or prom dresses for those for whom such a thing would ordinarily be out of reach, etc. Some needs are more urgent than others, of course, and some require more skill, more expertise, more hands, and more money than others do.

The Cultural Context for Mission

As this is being written, the United States is experiencing more polarization—both political and cultural—than we are likely to have experienced in our lifetimes. Inequality—both in terms of economics and of political and cultural power—is growing every year. While we may offer verbal respect to the principle of "one person, one vote," the fact is that a smaller number of persons have, in effect, many more votes than the average citizen. Corporate "persons" have behind them resources that magnify the influence of a few at the expense of the many. One challenge for Christians is to take seriously the need to find tangible ways to amplify the voices of those who are most frequently not heard, in order that everybody has the chance to participate in shaping political and social decisions that affect the lives of all.

When Paul, after his conversion, sought the blessing of leaders of the church, they offered it. "They asked only one thing, that we remember the poor, which was actually what I was eager to do" (Gal 2:10). To "remember the poor" is not always or only a matter of charitable acts. In fact, seriously remembering the situation of the voiceless, powerless, and vulnerable—persons who are not always, strictly speaking, lacking an income—more appropriately leads to structural remedies. The church in mission can recognize the urgency of the need for systemic, structural remedies, and help to amplify the call for them.

Our time is also one in which the democratic forms we have taken for granted are being challenged all around the world and here at home. Authoritarianism is appealing to some, especially those who are endangered or feel at risk as societies and economies change. To call out authoritarian styles of leadership makes vulnerable the one who calls it out, perhaps, but for a people who have from the beginning confessed that Jesus, not Caesar, is Lord, we have no choice but to find a way.

It may be that the most difficult challenge of all is human-related global climate change. Because it is happening gradually, the front-page news upstages it as an issue, but climate change is affecting us more certainly every year. We can see tangible evidence in the intensity of storms, melting ice packs, and threats to crops. According to Genesis, God has given human beings the responsibility for exercising "dominion" over the natural world (Gen 1:26–30). That has unfortunately often been understood to imply that we have been divinely appointed to dominate, as though to exercise that domination heedlessly, as though we were not going to be held accountable.

"Dominion" might better be understood not as freedom to dominate, but as the responsibility, the obligation, to care for the creation, which belongs to God, to whom we are always accountable. Human beings are the stewards of the natural world, which does not permit the kinds of exploitation that threaten to destroy it or make it uninhabitable whether for ourselves or for plants and animals. In a culture in which human-influenced climate change has become a political issue, debate proceeds as though science-based evidence were irrelevant. Political commitments often lead the discussion, and those who have a high stake in fossil fuels may have the loudest voices. Ecumenical Christians must join with others to engage the discussion without being distracted by the ideological baggage of partisan politics. Stewardship of the created world is a theological issue at bottom, involving the interrelatedness of the whole creation. A missional priority might be to engage in the discussion by leading with our strength, which is to contribute a broadly theological imperative to be stewards of what God has entrusted to all of us.

Reciprocity

Churches engage in various mission initiatives—or support the projects of others—because this is what God means for us to do simply because they need to be done. Mission projects are not meant to be covert ways of offering some good, desirable, or essential thing of value in exchange for the recipient's signing the membership roll. Nor are they meant to draw attention to our benevolence or to the abundance of resources that may be available for us to distribute. Neither are they occasions for advancing the interests of one ideology or one political party in a contest with another. We are meant to serve only one Lord. At the same time, to engage in these mission actions may suggest, to any who may be curious, what sort of God we have pledged to serve. And, known to us but probably not to those who are being served, mission action reflects our longing for the just and healing rebalancing we have seen represented in the vision of the *basileia*, God's purpose for the whole world.

A positive side effect of the many years in which "missions" were understood to be evangelizing people from every nation is that the missionaries came home to report their experiences. In the course of their reporting, Americans began to learn about places that seemed, at the time, far away and exotic, but in which there live real human beings. Church congregations, viewing the missionaries' slides and hearing their accounts, began to recognize the humanity of people in the Congo, or China, Indonesia, or India. They learned about climates, local customs, dress, arts, ways of governing, trade, and international politics in a time when information about such things was not readily available to the average person. In some cases, the missionaries arranged for local people among whom they worked overseas to come to visit American congregations to tell their own stories, or to enroll in denominational colleges, raising the consciousness of teachers and classmates as well as establishing friendships. These various efforts helped to lay a foundation for serious American interest in internationalism.

Mission at its best is reciprocal, in the sense that it is about forming relationships, often across social and geographical boundaries. In healthy relationships, it is not a matter of one party being the giver and the other the receiver, but each gives and each receives. The youth who participate in the mission trip to repaint a house in Appalachia or dig a well in Haiti come back with something they have received. It may be a broader perspective on the way various environmental and economic factors shape the terms of people's working and personal lives as well as either expanding or limiting their choices and opportunities. It may be the recognition that there are appealing ways of life and work that do not conform to the patterns to which the mission team are accustomed. It may be to learn that there can be grace and dignity in accepting the help of others when help is needed, or that hospitality can take many forms. Often it involves the recognition that people who may have been imagined to be very different from ourselves may be essentially more similar than not.

Vulnerability

Perhaps the encounters that are part of many mission-related activities have helped to open Christians to the discovery that people who have simply been invisible to us, even in our own communities and family networks, need to be seen and valued for themselves without being understood as projects to be worked on. To become acquainted with a person up close can help us to lay aside stereotypes and prejudices, and to recognize that differences, however unfamiliar, are simply variations on a single human theme.

To be engaged in mission can be imperialistic, insensitive, and arrogant; but it can also be quite the opposite. To be faithful requires that we risk empathy, aware that we have in common with others both neediness and repertoires of gifts to be celebrated and shared. To be a disciple of Jesus Christ requires a willingness to learn how to allow oneself to be vulnerable, when it seems that the goal of mainstream culture is, rather, to insulate us from vulnerability. The goal should not be reckless vulnerability; not inviting others to kick us or exploit us. Not the kind of vulnerability that begs for attention, sympathy, or praise, but the kind of vulnerability that accompanies advocacy for another who is vulnerable, though not by choice. Such vulnerability will always run the risk of being wrong and of overestimating ourselves and the reach of our good intentions. God is merciful, and can work in, through, and around our misshapen efforts, if necessary. Nevertheless, Christian mission of the sort that requires that our team be offered deference, recognition, special privilege, and exemptions unavailable to others is not recognizably Christian at all. There is already quite enough Christian triumphalism on display in the U.S., stemming from a fearful and defensive reflex that wants to hold on to a dominance that is fast receding. Reaching for control and status is not good for anyone, and it is notoriously bad for communities of faith.

Vulnerability and timidity are not the same thing. Vulnerability and shamefacedness are not the same thing. One can be bold, determined, and vulnerable at the same time in the execution of the church's communally shared and appointed role to be a priestly people—whose intercession, advocacy, and servanthood are meant to be extended in contribution to the mission of the blessing of "all the families of the earth" (Gen 12:3; Rev 5:10).

A lot of what churches do under the label of "mission" can be done and often is done by groups other than churches. A person in need of a meal for the family does not much care whether it comes from a church or an independent food bank or from members of a community service club.

To share a bag of groceries will probably not lead to a conversion on the part of the recipient. In fact, it may be just the opposite: the one volunteering in the soup kitchen, when deeply involved enough to meet a recipient on level ground, may be the one who experiences the conversion—a change of heart.

So, what does it matter? Churches collect canned goods, host a rotating meal for those experiencing food scarcity or just plain lonely, send a check to support the radio station that reads for the blind and visually impaired, distribute turkeys at Thanksgiving, and so might the local Kiwanis or Rotary Club. What matters is not whether the beneficiaries know who the donors are, much less that they understand the givers' motivations. What matters is that the church understand that our own various forms of benevolent outreach are rooted in a theological foundation. That foundation is not so much a set of ideas or ideals as it is a specific person: Jesus Christ.

The Ultimate Theological Foundation for Mission: Jesus Christ

In Jesus Christ, God has crossed a boundary, identifying with human beings who, by comparison with the deity, are always vulnerable, no matter how much power one has, or how much money stowed away. In our baptism, Christ has united us with him, which means union with him not only in his church, but in his solidarity with the vulnerable and the abused. The Christ to whom we have been joined by baptism and by faith unites us with him and one another in the work of holy priesthood—intercession and advocacy. The church is not an end in itself. Nor is it a club for those who expect to be going to heaven. The church is nothing less than a priestly community whose purpose is to represent, as best as it can, something of God's deep interest in the welfare of the whole human family. God's deep interest in the whole human family becomes evident in Christ, the healer and reconciler, whose ministry is but a foretaste of God's future, feeding our desire for the *basileia* that will one day fill the whole earth.

The work of the church includes committing itself to the continuing process of forming its members, shaping and reshaping us so that we may grow in the ability to discover our neighbors and include them in the circle of those for whom we give a damn. To be a Christian is to live into a lifelong process of conversion that is never finished until, in death, we complete our baptism. We who are the baptized find ourselves in the curious position of sharing in mentoring responsibilities while also in perpetual need of being mentored ourselves. Our personal formation is always incomplete and ongoing. At the same time, we participate in the communal responsibility of supporting the shared mentoring tasks that are basic to the identity of the church. We, the baptized, *are* the church, after all.

That mentoring process, in which we find ourselves to be counted among both the mentors and the mentees, has proved to be an environment in which failures and disappointments are not rare. As the church we share responsibility for its failures and disappointments, and on occasion have felt ourselves among those whom the church has failed and disappointed. Just as Jesus' disciples made themselves scarce when the temple police came to arrest him, it is easy enough for us to become spiritually AWOL precisely at the moment when our presence is most needed. We may love and honor the church while fully aware that the flawed humanity exhibited both individually and in communities has not been washed away by our baptism and is not absent from the church and our own experience. Amy Plantinga Pauw observes that "God's creative and redemptive purposes are worked out in the sometimes tragic ambiguities of concrete, creaturely communities."[3]

The church does not engage in mission in order to chalk up credits in heaven. It engages in mission for the same reason that it offers its worship: because, however dimly, we have seen that truth, insofar as we are able to see it, is God, as God has been made known in Christ by the Spirit. The God whose intention has been to make the divine self known is a God of justice. The biblical images of the *basileia* call upon us to employ our imagining skills for the purpose of picturing an ultimate future characterized not only by mending, healing, and reconciliation, but also by justice. If there is to be justice that is far-reaching enough to be worthy of the name, it will certainly require judgment.

Judgment/Justice

"Judgment" is one of those words rarely heard in many churches these days. It seems to be too evocative of the judgmentalism of which we have been accused, not always falsely, and that flourishes in many circles, both ecclesiastical and secular. Judging one another is a perpetual human temptation,

3. Plantinga Pauw, *Church in Ordinary Time*, 36.

but one that needs to be reined in. Nevertheless, when speaking specifically of God's judgment, we have to do not with capricious or mean-spirited judgments altogether too characteristic of human beings. We are speaking of divine judgment, a sacred action that is indispensable to true justice, and certainly to ultimate justice.

It will not be as though God will bring judgment to some, while for others there will be mercy. There will be both judgment and mercy for all, executed by the only One capable of balancing them perfectly. Judgment and mercy are two movements within the same act of grace. Judgment identifies wrongs done without asking those who have suffered from those wrongs to pretend they didn't happen. Judgment acknowledges and respects victims of wrong, including those who have been the victims not of other human beings, but also of natural catastrophes: earthquake, wind, flood, and fire, including those, like Noah's flood, that have been attributed to God. Judgment is necessary because it does not permit papering over huge injustices as though they never happened, because the evidence that they have happened is that they always leave indelible marks on their victims (John 20:27).

God's judgment, unlike many human judgments, is not vindictive, but loving. It is loving because it takes us all seriously, and takes seriously the harm we have done as well as experienced. It is loving because it honors our need to recognize such harm ourselves and have it called by name. The remedy for it is not forgetfulness, but forgiveness. God's judgment is loving because it is saturated in mercy. No one is exempt from the need to be held accountable, whether for what we have done or for what we have left undone. It is necessary, ultimately, for the sake of justice that we see ourselves with blinders off.

And yet, there is mercy. Mercy unearned, not paid for by us or owed to us. God's judgment is gracious, and God's grace begins, as it must, with a brutally honest assessment. Yet, the grace of judgment has been foreseen in our baptism, which is already a kind of death by drowning as well as an anticipation of resurrection. In our baptism we have met Christ, been judged and died with him, been flooded with his grace. Our baptism is God's pledge and assurance that God's judgment is not intended to curse or annihilate us, but to declare that in spite of the sins common to mortals, God does not reject us, but is readying us for a place in a new creation.

This-Worldly Spirituality

The church in mission on this side of the *basileia* is meant to exhibit our longing, in a manner however flawed, for the ultimate justice toward which the whole creation is groaning—a state of being in which judgment and grace are one, and everything is brought into balance. Justice and vulnerability go together. The Christian gospel is, in the end, not so much about looking for some sort of generic "spiritual experience." Pastor and martyr Dietrich Bonhoeffer saw "a religiosity of inwardness as a betrayal of God's call to this creaturely way of life . . ." and affirms "the profound this-worldliness of Christianity."[4] Nor is the gospel about an unspoiled tranquility, leaving us untouched and undisturbed, walled off and immunized from the suffering of the world.

The way of discipleship is not always peaceful and not always an upbeat spiritual experience. To be a Christian is first and foremost to be a disciple of Jesus. While most of our energy will no doubt need to be devoted to taking care of ourselves and those closest to us for whom we are particularly responsible, to be a disciple sometimes means washing feet, so to speak. Sometimes providing words for those who have no words, or at least have no words that are being heard. Perhaps helping to make visible those who have been invisible. Sometimes it will be crossing boundaries to introduce strangers to each other. Sometimes it means sharing the lot of the vulnerable, even, once in a while, the vulnerable guilty.

Even though the church, in its thorough humanity, will sometimes fail to be what it has been called to be, discipleship is by definition and by necessity a shared effort, a communal affair. The Christian life is not typically one of solitude, even should we be among those who spend much of our lives alone. Even the desert fathers and mothers prayed with the whole communion of saints very much in mind.

Faith waxes and it wanes, and is particularly vulnerable when it seems that so many persons whom we respect and admire have either abandoned faith or never possessed it. We need each other, and need to share our perceptions of the challenges of faith and meet them in mutual support. The Lord's Day assembly provides us with spiritual food and drink that is a kind of "knowing"; and mission in, to, and for the world engages us in ways that reinforce such "knowing." In both instances—worship and mission—we commit to attachment rather than detachment.

---

4. Plantinga Pauw, *Church in Ordinary Time*, 16, 17.

The church in this time remains the only community on earth entrusted with communicating what we have received in the gospel. Careful and experienced listening is a primary skill if we are not to misrepresent that with which the church has been entrusted. Sometimes that calls for words, for conversation that can be had at a level of a reasonable, prudent, and generous detachment; for finding speech that is common speech rather than presupposing familiarity with the special language of the church. But that sort of conversation ought to be offered when wanted, while never imposed.

Front Porches

There still exist people who, should it be possible for obstacles to be cleared away in a reasoned exchange, are truly interested in knowing more about this faith. Someone has suggested that what the churches need is something like a front porch—some meeting place that is genuinely neutral, not a covert effort to sign people up. Whether organized or not organized, ordinary human exchanges often begin when people are experiencing times of transition and really need to think it through with someone: when there may be a new member of the family, empty nest, job change, a move from one community to another, retirement, illness, graduation, not to mention the various adjustments required when there are changes in the social and political climate. Front porch conversation should not be manipulative, but engaged without a pre-conceived notion that it must be made to lead to one end or another. Exploring issues of faith is a risk—one better taken only in response to one who sincerely wants to engage with us about it.

Spending an evening wandering around the city of Lausanne, Switzerland, on a Saturday night, this writer was surprised to come upon a church with its front doors wide open, lights on, and a couple of people inside prepared to welcome the curious, show them the worship space if they wished, willing to engage in conversation if questions should be asked, but not required or forced. Those who wanted only to take a look were welcome to do it on their own without interference. One image, I think, of a kind of front porch. There have to be other front porches as well, and surely there are among us a sufficient number of creative people to imagine what they might look like. An essential aspect of mission is to tailor it to circumstances, but we who have heard the royal commission, "Go therefore . . ." still need to figure out ways to do it gently, responsibly, and fittingly.

For Christians to recommit ourselves to those areas of interest that fit in a general category describable as mission, the first challenge would seem to be enabling congregations and participants to embrace a deeper understanding of what they are about. It is not so difficult to get people to sign up for projects that involve doing good, whether at church or a service club. The projects may look very much the same, in any case, but they will necessarily be understood somewhat differently. That difference requires exploring both the theological basis of mission in its several aspects (including the challenge of how to share the gospel in respectful ways) and at the same time studying the current social and cultural settings that need to be taken into account. Most Christians sense that we have entered a new era, that circumstances have changed for churches, and would welcome a conversation about it. Out of earnest study and sharing of insights, new ways of reaching out may well be discovered, tested, sorted, and shared. They will not all come from experts, denominational offices, or ordained officers.

8

Is Faith Still Possible?

"And yet, when the Son of man comes, will he find faith on earth?"
— LUKE 18:8b

Will It Always Be Thursday?

NOTICE HOW THE TITLE question of this chapter is phrased. Not, "Is it possible for ecumenical churches to recover their privileged standing in our society?" Nor, "Is it possible for us to maintain our churches and institutions more or less as they are?" The question asks, rather, whether *faith* is still possible. And, given the context, the "faith" presumed in the question is, in one sense, the shared faith for which the historic churches, Catholic, Protestant, and Orthodox, have understood themselves to be responsible stewards. And in another sense, the "faith" in question is the possibility of a person cultivating a confident trust in the God who has reached out to human beings in Christ and the Spirit.

History makes it evident enough that predicting long-term likelihoods based on short-term trends is not always reliable. If it should seem obvious that the future will deliver even more of what we are seeing now, we shall likely be proved wrong. So, it is a fool's errand to try to project from today's data just how the historic churches will fare in the long run. Even so, we are wise to consider that the ecumenical churches are not likely to regain the virtual monopoly they experienced throughout most of American history.

It would also be prudent to work with the presumption that our congregations, denominations, and institutions will have to adapt to a significantly new situation. And our situation, most likely, will be that of a minority community in a society shared with many other minority communities. So, "Is faith still possible?" is a question driven by the probability that, if faith should prove to be still possible, it will be a faith that does not draw its energy from large-scale public acquaintance, interest, and support.

The bigger question is whether our cultural environment has evolved to the point that Christian faith is literally impossible for a thoughtful person who is paying attention. No question that those of us who embrace it feel that our faith is being challenged, for a variety of reasons. We have already noted how easy and natural it is for a Christian to feel embarrassed when we encounter public figures, radio preachers, and would-be theocrats whose use of Jesus-talk seems clumsy, often alien, and sometimes downright hostile. Such embarrassing language encourages scornful skeptics, whose rejection of all faith claims seems to be based on a growing consensus that faith is self-serving, narrowly exclusive, and a kind of magical thinking. Challenges from both of these directions are real, and unless we simply give up under the pressure, we shall have to learn how to meet them. If not, every day will certainly be a Thursday!

But even if there were no aggressive fundamentalisms trying to repeal the modern world, and if there were fewer and/or less dismissive voices of skepticism, the dominant culture itself provokes a challenge to faith. Summing up many of the main points already made throughout this book, consider again that what is taken to be reasonable and believable by the dominant culture is not new, nor a product of the twentieth or twenty-first centuries. Today's dominant culture has been shaped by an old movement, one well known and represented by esteemed figures such as Emmanuel Kant and Thomas Jefferson. The Enlightenment (or Age of Reason) has been expanding its influence for centuries, and in the process crowded out alternative voices. At first taking root mainly in intellectual circles, a triumphant rationalism has now filtered down to virtually everyone, including people who go to church. The technological successes produced by the scientific method have rewarded its enabling philosophy with an authority presumed to extend to every corner of human experience.

Prove It!

Curiously, it is now, at the zenith of its public success, that the underlying foundations of the Enlightenment can no longer be presumed to be immune from questioning. The Enlightenment and Newtonian physics work together, hand in hand; but the day of Newtonian physics has passed. Quantum physics raises questions about scientific certainties long presumed to be unquestionable. One of these days, it may even become less intimidating for alternative voices at least to work into the conversation an occasional "Yes, but . . ." The centuries-long era shaped by the Enlightenment is in process of being reshaped in ways not entirely predictable, but the public is largely unaware of it. We have all digested the by now venerable lesson that a claim of any kind meant to be taken seriously needs to be challenged with a demand to "Prove it!" And proving it must always mean proving it by means of something like an objective, arms-length, data-driven method. In other words, proof requires demonstrating that the claim can be verified within the terms specified by the rules of the currently dominant culture.

No problem, of course, when we are talking about phenomena that can be studied by direct observation or by employing indirect methods such as mathematical formulas and computer simulations. But, it must be insisted, God is not a phenomenon within the universe, but its Creator. "Knowledge" of God is not available by any combination of scientific or philosophical investigations. If human beings are to "know" God by any means at all, it will be on God's terms.

People of faith are likely to believe that the universe itself, God's own artifact, suggests God, but it is a suggestion—not proof in the scientific sense—and it does not mean that the universe cannot be seen quite differently. Faith in God arises, if at all, not exclusively or even primarily out of a process of reasoning, but making use of an in-born repertoire of sensors for which the dominant culture offers little respect. We have, in effect, put into storage parts of ourselves whose function is meant to serve as a kind of internal compass. The compass is intended to alert us to invisible realities that subtly beckon for our attention, but are neither specific nor subject to scientific investigation. Engaging a larger reality with the help of the intuitive sense should reasonably be subject to questioning (just as virtually every claim should be subject to questioning). However, a conviction that takes hold assisted by the energy of an intuitive insight need not be automatically discredited, whether having to do with faith, or science, either one.

As pointed out in an earlier chapter, intuition—a kind of precognitive but not unreasonable "sense"—serves a purpose even in the practice of science. It also serves non-scientific purposes, other ways of sensing, apprehending, even "knowing" that are indispensable if we are to find our way reliably in an often overwhelming universe. Overwhelming because we are literally impacted at every moment by more incoming data than we can possibly process consciously. And much of it in forms not easily organized in a narrowly intellectual fashion.

In other words, to manage these masses of data in some organized way sufficient to guide us in living a life attuned to its deepest rhythms, we need some help. Help manifests itself in a variety of ways, including intellectual sorting out. In that process as well as in others, Christians believe that God is at work to provide such help, such empowering, by the Holy Spirit. This is not magic, but the conviction that God is showing us a way, though it may sometimes seem less than orderly, and is often exercised by indirection. The Spirit works however it will, often in and through communities, and always relationally. The Spirit may be made manifest in and through the ways we learn to hear and tell the stories we have received—narratives that serve to identify the Spirit we sense to be at work in and among us. Narratives typically drawn from profound communal experience often energized and supported by a sensible and shared intuition—the ability to imagine what we cannot see.

It is not true to presume that we in the twenty-first century are the heirs of so much more knowledge than any of our forebears that God has been reduced to the status of an obsolete notion, a leftover from a naïve and ignorant childhood of the race. To believe that we have outgrown God requires bowing to the dominant cultural bias that the only answers that count, whatever the questions, are the answers that can be provided by science, or something *science-ish*. This perception of scientific omniscience is a projection that a lay public imposes on science. Those most steeped in scientific principles, in contrast, know the limits of their discipline. Some things that are worth knowing, even urgent to know, are not processed best by the reasoning intellect alone. Like so many other worthy things, these cannot be known with a claim of absolute certainty, or proven to a skeptic.

Before I become too attached to my own argument, a notation is in order. The question of just how we can claim to "know" anything is one we can hardly avoid, but reasoning takes us only so far. After all is said and done, God is not a problem to be solved. God is not subject to being subpoenaed to appear on the witness stand to produce credentials that will satisfy our scrutiny. The living God does not need our defensive arguments. God reaches out to us without much interest in our curious speculations about the divine methods. But, as the old camp song goes, "When he [sic] calls me, I will answer."

Yes, of Course . . .

So, yes, of course, faith is still possible—faith of all sorts, but, for our interests, specifically Christian faith. Faith is still possible, clearly enough, if for no other reason that it has not ceased to exist, even in places where it has long been out of fashion. Nor is it limited to those with few intellectual resources. And it will not cease to exist unless God wills that it should. To cite his words to disciples once again, Jesus said, "You did not choose me but I chose you" (John 15:16).

For a person to whom God is more than a concept, an idea to be entertained with more or less interest, it is almost inconceivable to imagine being talked out of one's faith. In any context, one is not likely to be talked out of whatever or whomever one has come to love. Ideas can be let go, convictions can be reconsidered, but even should one be absolutely overwhelmed with a barrage of persuasive arguments, one does not easily put away the object of one's love. Misunderstandings abound, and being wrong is possible, and one can be backed into a corner with an argument, but love perseveres. One's faith follows and attaches to whatever/whomever one has come to love. So, yes, faith is and shall remain possible no matter the changing landscapes.

To repeat a theme of this book, faith involves a conversion of the imagination. If the dominant Enlightenment-shaped culture has insisted that it is not possible to address any serious issue without using analytic, detached language to establish and prove the argument, then we are left with no useful language to speak of God. When we read the Bible expecting textbook language, we are led almost inevitably to skepticism. Skepticism is a state of mind we have all at least visited.

Paul Ricoeur, a French philosopher/theologian, has suggested the possibility of moving beyond skepticism, so easily acquired. He describes such a move as discovering a "second naiveté."[1] That sounds right to me. After all, our first naiveté, usually originating in childhood, isn't enough to

---

1. Ricoeur, *The Symbolism of Evil*, 351.

sustain us as we outgrow it. Things learned in Sunday school or children's sermons may very well be among those things we once accepted naively and easily enough, only to find implausible as we mature and encounter the intellectual framework that dominates school and culture. But, experience shows that it is possible

> to revisit the image, symbol, or idea and ponder it, reflect on it, walk around it in order to view it from various angles and discover that it is much larger, much more profound than one might have thought either in the first, naive encounter, or in the skeptical mode.[2]

To embrace a second naiveté will involve recognizing that the story, symbol, image or idea we had come to reject had, in our first naiveté, been framed too woodenly, been too flattened out, too indifferent to the nuances that might provide access to its liveliness. In other words, it is possible to experience a conversion of the imagination: to encounter a story, an image that we thought we had understood, then found wanting and rejected, only to discover that it is "larger, much roomier, than we had imagined in the first [naïve] encounter . . . more spacious and hospitable than it had seemed to be when a necessary skepticism had seemed to narrow it."[3]

The numbers of the faithful may be fewer in years to come, when there will be few incentives just to go along with the program. But one might reasonably predict that those who do profess the faith (likely with the help of a second naiveté) will be likely to do it with a deliberation that often accompanies minority status. To cultivate that deliberation will require re-thinking the responsibility of being a teaching and mentoring church, and the lifelong project of helping each other grow in faith, drawing upon its inexhaustible resources. We shall likely have to do without the presumption that these tasks will require little effort, come easily, or be rewarded by the admiration of society.

It may be that, in the near future at least, church life will not look entirely different than it does now. In Europe, which has been immersed in skeptical rationalism longer and more intensively than the U.S., churches have closed, others host smaller congregations than before, and most people do not attend worship except, perhaps, on rare occasions. And yet, if one has worshiped in England, Scotland, France, Germany, Switzerland,

---

2. Byars, *Sacraments in Biblical Perspective*, 15.

3. Byars, *Sacraments in Biblical Perspective*, 15.

the Scandinavian countries, it is clear that the Christian faith has not ceased to exist. Not all congregations are small. Not all the worshipers are old. After people sort themselves out, there remain those who are faithful. They do not appear to be intimidated by their minority status. They have adapted to a situation that is, historically, relatively recent, and are making the best of it. Gifted women and men still prepare for ministry. The people who continue to worship regularly do not spend much energy whining about a lost era. Bitterness serves no cause well. Faith appears to be sustainable even when the larger society is indifferent.

In the Netherlands, more than two-thirds of the population is unchurched, and yet, the Protestant Church in the Netherlands is not content just to continue in existence, but is actively engaged in trying to reach out to the local culture. Motivated by a sense of mission rather than a comprehensive strategy, churches are using even their sanctuaries as meeting-places for neighbors. These spaces, suggestive of the holy, evoke a sense of transcendence even when the gathering may be only for a current film. And, over the last eight years, the church "has started 84 church plants— 'pioneering places,' as the church calls them—as new expressions of Christian community for people who don't belong to existing congregations."[4]

Some Helpful Role Models

In the U.S., in places and situations where one might be bold enough to ask non-conforming strangers, neighbors, or even relatives an intimate question, that question might once have been, "Why don't you go to church?" That question is, in most parts of the country, obsolete. The new one for non-conforming acquaintances, if one should be so bold as to ask, might be, "Why *do* you go to church?" No doubt European Christians have had to ponder a response to such a question, even if only to feel as though they might be prepared to answer it should occasion require. One would hope that, in a society where such a question conceivably might be asked, one would have thought about what to say. I suspect that when Christians finally absorb the fact that they are, whatever the official numbers, a cultural minority, they will tutor themselves to be able to offer a coherent response. Those who participate in worship regularly will find themselves needing and wanting to answer the question "Why do this?" at least for themselves, even if no one is likely ever to ask them directly.

4. Van Driel, *Post-Christian Lessons*, 30.

Muslims who live in Dearborn, Michigan, or Lexington, Kentucky, can't help but be aware that the larger culture doesn't know much about who they are, and they may find themselves unprepared to explain their religious identity. After all, in Egypt or Iraq that identity could be taken for granted. Needing to have a sense of why they are what they are, they are often motivated to investigate their inherited faith more carefully and energetically, and sometimes even more zealously than had they not felt led to do so by the self-consciousness that goes with minority status. Christians will likely not feel their minority status quite as keenly as the Muslim or the Hindu, but they will be sufficiently aware of it that they may feel a similar need to be able to explain their own faith, if only for their own peace of mind. If that should be the case, future congregations are likely to include many who will be eager to learn—a fact that will likely shape expectations of future pastors, preachers, mentors, guides, catechists, and educators trained for the purpose.

It is possible to imagine that congregations that become smaller as their aging constituents die off may eventually be composed of a remaining core of younger people. That fact will pose a challenge to shape congregational life in ways appropriate to their developing constituencies. Opportunities for learning, mission, worship, and community formation may well be pared down and more tightly focused for members and inquirers who have to prioritize and budget their time.

New Occasions Teach New Duties

Some of the more one-sided characteristics of the centuries-old Enlightenment are now burning out. It is not likely that Western societies will cease to value being rational, but rationalism (reducing experience exclusively to objective/analytic thought processes) will less often be able to eclipse altogether some other ways of "knowing" that which is deeply real. Molly Worthen, writing specifically about evangelicals, observed that

> for some evangelicals, a stronger sense of participation in holy mystery offers a metaphysical jolt to the system—at a time when the relationship between evangelical worship and politics seems broken . . . All these people have one thing in common: the instinct that worship should be an act of humility, not hubris . . . But

the effort must also advance at the precognitive level, in the habits
and relationships of worshiping communities.[5]

In other words, the assembly for worship needs to be more than a
forum for either reasoned or passionate arguments centering on politics or
cultural conflicts or, I would add, simply explaining holy things as though
they could be reduced to a set of ideas. Worship is about an encounter with
the holy that is, as Worthen suggests, "precognitive." Not anti-cognitive, not
anti-intellectual, but neither confined to the analytic exercise of the mind
alone. Rather, the precognitive makes use of capacities that we have been
persuaded, out of an acquired cultural suspicion of them, to deactivate,
more or less. Western culture has cultivated a suspicion of any serious conviction that might be suspected of being fueled to any extent by emotion.
The approved message warns us all to resist impulses to trust feelings, thus
privileging the coldly rational. "Coldly" meaning scrubbed free of any trace
of personal engagement, preferring to trust a stance presumably rooted in
personal indifference.[6]

Ecumenical Christians, embarrassed by fundamentalisms and up-
staged by reasonable skeptics, may identify too eagerly with the less-em-
barrassing skeptics. In other words, inadvertently appear to be trying to
solve our problems by, maybe, just toning down a little any talk of Jesus
Christ—the same Christ whom we share with those whose narrowness
and triumphalism embarrass us. Any such toning down comes close to
handing over Jesus Christ to sectarians who are desperate to hold on to
(usually white) Protestant hegemony. It wouldn't be the first time church
people found Jesus Christ to be burdensome if the object is to win popular
approval. History demonstrates that it is possible to have something like
a church even when Christ is either missing altogether, or he is recast as
one more moralist, mystic, or revolutionary. (Just ask the novelist Flannery O'Connor.[7]) The temptation to minimize Christ's role in our faith will
have consequences, intended or not. Especially so should we imagine that

---

5. "How to Escape . . . "

6. Do you think it is purely an accident that "emotional" has acquired an association
with the feminine, and "rational" has been identified with the masculine? Or to suggest
a related link to the presumption that emotion is something to be distrusted, so that
decisions should be the privilege of those, male or female, presumed to be capable of
emotion-free rationality?

7. For example, the "Church without Christ," in O'Connor, *Wise Blood*.

setting him off to one side might serve to salvage our church in a time of triumphant skepticism.

If it should seem necessary to marginalize Christ to save his church, he'll need to call together another one. After all, whether Christianity is conceived as a movement or as an institution, its draw has been to the person of Jesus Christ first and foremost. Whatever might be salvaged should we turn away from our "true north" cannot be expected to please God or authentically represent the One who has marked us as his own—that One who cast his lot with us poor sinners in the first place.

Rather than giving up the treasure that, among many valuable things, is greatest of all, it is worth noting that not all who identify as "evangelical" are fundamentalist, or naïve, judgmental, or earnestly seeking to censor textbooks and seize public spaces for themselves. Some are simply looking for a Christian voice that is more than an echo of the dominant culture. They feel a need for substance, for serious engagement with the core affirmations of the faith, and that without embarrassment or apology. Perhaps they have not looked far enough to find that voice, those affirmations. Or it may be that we ecumenical folks have been too theologically timid to meet such reasonable expectations. It may be that an evangelical church has discerned their need and drawn their attention, while proving disappointing in other ways. Certainly a catholic voice in reforming mode is also capable of meeting a need for substance.

Ecumenical Christians would do well to consider the earnestness of those whose search is for God rather than ideology or cultural hegemony—including those who are searching for a language with which to speak about God. The language of ecumenical churches may be different than that of evangelicals, and our piety set in a different key, but it is a language and a piety rooted in a tradition that is both ancient and supple enough to challenge secular triumphalism. The Christian faith has moral and ethical implications, but it is more than a moral or ethical system. It has a healing element to it, but it is not only a method of healing. It is, at bottom, gospel—good news—anchored in the person of Jesus Christ, about whom we must speak in a manner that is rooted theologically in a generous and reforming catholicity. Substance matters.

And so, Now What?

It is more than time for ecumenical Christians to take notice of the elephant in the room: the elephant that everyone sees, from behind the pulpit as well as from the back pew, but that all seem to have quietly agreed not to notice. One can be active in some congregations without ever encountering even a little straight-forward attention to the challenges that we all feel intensely. So, believers on Sunday; nearly atheists by Thursday (thank you, Pastor Luckey for modeling how to *pay attention*). If we are to find a way to redeem even our Thursdays, it will require a good hard look at the elephant.

To prescribe strategies is to set oneself up for ridicule, but, based on current trends and observations, it seems as though some possible ways of engaging with the challenges of the moment might include something like:

- Relearning, if we have forgotten, how to deal directly with serious theological questions, and to spend more time and energy teaching congregations the essential rudiments of classic catholic Christianity as seen through Reformation and other reforming eyes. This will include directly calling out and addressing ways in which our culture as it has developed has privileged objective, analytic processes at the expense of other ways of engaging with the totality of experience. And, demonstrating alternative ways that language can be used to say what scientific or even journalistic language doesn't know how to say. It will also involve teaching the liturgy—not learning technical jargon, but reflecting on basic affirmations as they have been embedded and embodied devotionally and sacramentally in the classical forms. While we're at it, an even harder lesson: learning how to let go and allow ourselves to disarm our suspicions of ritual, relaxing our guardedness enough to enter the rites and go with the flow.

- Discovering various ways of spiritual formation that involve an opening of the self to God, however God might use the moment. For example, training people to serve as spiritual directors (not therapists, but coaching others to help them learn to discern how God may be speaking, acting, and nudging them as they examine their lives, relationships, and sense of vocation). *Lectio Divina*, centering prayer, and other disciplines can be useful in seeking to deepen a relationship with God. These do not exclude the kind of searches for God that are involved in the active use of the intellect in biblical, theological and related study that are themselves a way of loving and relating to God.

The future of a vital Christian life depends on our broadening the repertoire that demonstrates various paths that may lead to a deeper Christian spirituality to the end of making us more available to God and our neighbors.

- Where there are full-time pastors, job descriptions may need to be rewritten to serve different priorities than the busy CEO-like job descriptions typical today, among which will be far more extensive face-to-face teaching and mentoring, based not so much on a typical classroom model as on a variety of conversational patterns paced to suit learning intended to be internalized—made one's own—and necessarily scheduled in a variety of ways and diverse settings.[8]

- Where full-time pastors are not affordable, it will be necessary for ecclesiastical bodies to organize support for those who might serve part-time, perhaps several part-timers dividing a variety of very specifically identified specialties, such as teaching, overseeing mentoring groups, or discovering how to offer "front porch" conversations. Such support will include both personal oversight and guidance for those functioning in part-time pastoral, educational, or administrative roles, and providing continuing theological and liturgical nurturing.

- In urban areas or larger regions, it is likely that there will be one or more congregations that are larger and have more resources than most, including more than one staff member. It is possible that a denomination might work with such a congregation to help it develop a role of something like a "cathedral" church in the sense that it will serve in a kind of mothering role for the congregations of a city or region, based both on its more extensive resources along with resources pooled from among smaller congregations who will benefit.

- Recovery of Word and Eucharist. When the Eucharist is celebrated more than explained, it touches those parts of us that might be described by the word "precognitive," as Molly Worthen put it. Music, movement, gesture, posture, and actions can be adapted to suit a variety of cultures, but a challenge for subsequent generations is to reactivate the intuitive senses that we have held in suspicion, denied, and from which we have distanced ourselves in favor of the perfectly rational. The sacraments lend themselves to that challenge and,

8. For examples, see Batchelder, *Pathways;* and Wasserman, *Accompanying Newcomers.*

properly understood and practiced, will also support biblically-based preaching that functions sacramentally. Worship that suits the so-called "cathedral church" will, of course, look a little or a lot different than worship in the small congregation meeting in a borrowed room, while in substance each keeps faith with the other.

- Embracing a more intentional discipleship will involve a process over time of reimagining our identity in relation to cultural change. It will continue to be an enormous challenge to begin to think of ourselves other than as the unofficially appointed chaplains to the nation, with the special status and influence that once went with it. Jewish Americans have learned very well how to claim a place within mainstream society while understanding that, spiritually, they have to work out their identity from within their position as a minority. Even though ecumenical Christians may not be a small minority, we are likely to be a minority—certainly a cultural minority—and that requires learning to think like one, taking lessons, perhaps, from our Jewish, Muslim, and Hindu sisters and brothers. That challenge may help us to read the New Testament with deeper appreciation, since the Christians of the first two centuries were certainly a minority trying to live out their faith commitment without the blessing of the dominant culture. Of course, learning how to be a minority in a pre-Christian society is different from learning it in a post-Christian society. However, although circumstances in the first or second century were different from ours in the twenty-first, there are parallels. Both require the kind of self-awareness that makes it possible to discern the points at which the gospel and the prevailing culture are easily compatible and where they are at odds, and working out how to be counter-cultural as required in various situations. To be counter-cultural—i.e., not picking quarrels, but keeping priorities in order—invites a measure of vulnerability and calls for a lot of mutual support.

Indeed, when Pastor Luckey preached his sermon contrasting our Sundays with our Thursdays, it was to remind us that one can't be a Christian all alone, even should we be physically separated from one another. We need the support of the community of the faithful more than we have at any time in our living memories.

Caveats

One of the risks of a minority frame of mind is that the minority may begin to think of itself in terms of victimhood and push back with a strategy of general hostility to the dominant culture. Another risk is the temptation to sectarianism—erecting walls between the group and those outside, dividing those in from those out. Or, perhaps less risky but equally self-destructive, the minority may lose interest in the larger world beyond the group, focusing only on its own inner life. While a minority—whether numerically or culturally—does need to understand its own reason for existence as clearly as possible, it needs at the same time to balance that with general openness to the world. This is tricky, but the gospel, rightly understood, leads us in exactly that direction. One simply cannot understand Jesus Christ without perceiving the ways that he crossed boundaries, and one cannot understand Israel and its Bible without taking account of the prophetic voices that critiqued their own community.

Catholicity of the sort that is sympathetic and appreciative of historical reform movements, does not reject the world as such, but understands it to be the object of God's love. That being the case, the world is meant to be the object of the church's love as well, notwithstanding the world's exasperating complexity. God promised Abram that his progeny would become a great nation, to the end that "in you all the families of the earth shall be blessed" (Gen 12:3). That is Israel's mission, and the church's, in season and out of season. This is God's mission, the one with which God will certainly enable those who are receptive to it to keep faith.

When some of those in the wider circle that had followed Jesus found that to follow him further was a bridge too far, they turned back. Turning to the twelve, Jesus asked, "Do you also wish to go away?" Simon Peter, who often served as spokesperson for them all, replied, "Lord, to whom can we go? You have the words of eternal life" (John 6:68).

In our society there are many "words" on offer, some of them attractive, even persuasive. The dominant culture itself, unofficially but also unavoidably, favors some "words" over others. Jesus' question to the twelve makes it clear enough that, should we wish to drop out, turn back, go away, embrace some other "word," we are free to do that. But for some, the reply to his question will always—always—be "Lord, to whom shall we go? You have the words of eternal life."

The late Hans Frei, describing H. Richard Niebuhr's theological legacy, wrote that Niebuhr would have asserted . . . that our responsibility to affirm the glory of the Lord, and his glory alone, has not been altered one whit, and that this remains our duty in propitious or unpropitious times.[9]

9. Frei, *Theology & Narrative*, 231.

Bibliography

Batchelder, David B. *Pathways to the Waters of Grace: A Guide for a Church's Ministry with Parents Seeking Baptism for their Children.* Eugene, OR: Wipf & Stock, 2017.

Byars, Ronald P. *Finding Our Balance: Repositioning Mainstream Protestantism.* Eugene, OR: Cascade Books, 2015.

———. *The Sacraments in Biblical Perspective.* Interpretation: Resources for the Use of Scripture in the Church. Louisville: Westminster John Knox, 2011.

Calvin, John. *Institutes of the Christian Religion.* Edited by John T. McNeill. 2 vols. Library of Christian Classics 20–21. Philadelphia: Westminster, 1960.

Frei, Hans W. "H. Richard Niebuhr on History, Church, and Nation." In *Theology & Narrative: Selected Essays*, edited by George Hunsinger and William C. Placher, 213–33. New York: Oxford University Press, 1993.

Hays, Richard B. *The Conversion of the Imagination: Paul as Interpreter of Israel's Scripture.* Grand Rapids: Eerdmans, 2005.

Jenson, Robert W. *Canon and Creed.* Interpretation: Resources for the Use of Scripture in the Church. Louisville: Westminster John Knox, 2010.

Johnson, Luke Timothy. *Miracles: God's Presence and Power in Creation.* Interpretation: Resources for the Use of Scripture in the Church. Louisville: Westminster John Knox, 2018.

———. *The Revelatory Body: Theology as Inductive Art.* Grand Rapids: Eerdmans, 2015.

Kuhn, Thomas S. *The Structure of Scientific Revolutions.* 2nd ed. Chicago: University of Chicago Press, 1970.

Lathrop, Gordon W. *The Four Gospels on Sunday: The New Testament and the Reform of Christian Worship.* Minneapolis: Fortress, 2012.

———. *Saving Images: The Presence of the Bible in Christian Liturgy.* Minneapolis: Fortress, 2017.

Long, Thomas G. "The Binary Christianity of Marcus Borg." *Christian Century* 134/15 (July 19, 2017). https://www.christiancentury.org/review/binary-christianity-of-marcus -borg/.

O'Connor, Flannery. *Wise Blood.* New York: Farrar, Straus & Giroux, 1962.

O'Donnell, Emma. *Remembering the Future: The Experience of Time in Jewish and Christian Liturgy.* Collegeville, MN: Liturgical, 2015.

Plantinga Pauw, Amy. *Church in Ordinary Time: A Wisdom Ecclesiology.* Grand Rapids: Eerdmans, 2017.

Presbyterian Church (USA). *Book of Common Worship.* Louisville: Westminster John Knox, 1993.

Bibliography

———. *Glory to God: The Presbyterian Hymnal*. Louisville: Westminster John Knox, 2013.

Read, David H. C. *Preacher: David H. C. Read's Sermons at Madison Avenue Presbyterian Church*. Edited by John McTavish. Eugene, OR: Wipf & Stock, , 2017.

Ricoeur, Paul. *The Symbolism of Evil*. Translated by Emerson Buchanan.. Religious Perspectives 17. New York: Harper & Row, 1967.

Routledge, Clay. "Don't Believe in God? Maybe You'll Try U.F.O.s." *New York Times*, Sunday Review, July 21, 2017. https://www.nytimes.com/2017/07/21/opinion/sunday/dont-believe-in-god-maybe-youll-try-ufos.html

Saint-Exupéry, Antoine de. *Le Petit Prince*. New York: Harcourt Brace Jovanovich, 1943.

Schmemann, Alexander. *The Eucharist: Sacrament of the Kingdom*. Crestwood, New York: St. Vladimir's Seminary Press, 2000.

Taylor-Hall, Mary Ann. *Come and Go, Molly Snow*. New York: Norton, 1995.

United Church of Christ. *Book of Worship: United Church of Christ*. New York: Office for Church Life and Leadership, 1986.

United Methodist Church. *The United Methodist Book of Worship*. Nashville: United Methodist Publishing House, 1992.

van Driel, Edwin Chr. "Ministering to the Grandchildren of the Lost Son: Post-Christian Lessons from Dutch Churches." *Presbyterian Outlook* 200/13 (September 17, 2018) 29–35.

Wasserman, Marney Ault. *Companions: Accompanying Newcomers into Church Life and Faith*. Eugene, OR: Wipf & Stock, 2016.

Worthen, Molly. "How to Escape from Roy Moore's Evangelicalism." *New York Times*, Sunday Review, November 17, 2017. https://www.nytimes.com/2017/11/17/opinion/sunday/escape-roy-moores-evangelicalism.html/.

Wright, N. T. *The Day the Revolution Began: Reconsidering the Meaning of Jesus's Crucifixion*. New York: HarperOne, 2016.